CONTE

ASSISTING THE SPIRITUALITY OF THE CHILD

Caring for the

Whole Child

A Holistic Approach
to Spirituality

The Children's Society
MAKING LIVES WORTH LIVING

John Bradford

First published in 1995 by
The Children's Society
Edward Rudolf House
Margery Street
London WC1X 0JL
Tel. 0171-837 4299

A catalogue record for this book is available from the British Library.

ISBN 0 907324 97 5

FOREWORD

Those of us who are parents will have often encountered searching questions from our children. Who am I? Why am I here? Where do I belong? What is the meaning of life? These are reflections of our children's spiritual journey, as important as their physical, mental and emotional growing up. As adults, our responses are based on our inherited and acquired values and beliefs. We try to enrich our children's lives, make new and varied opportunities available to them and help them to make sense of the world in which they are living. Our faith is something of value to pass on to them.

Children whose lives have been disrupted or difficult, or who have had to live away from their families, may sometimes miss out on this dimension of their development into young adults. The Government recognised the importance of the spiritual and religious needs of children when we drafted the Children Act. Translating such fundamental issues into practical reality is a far more difficult matter.

I am grateful that The Revd John Bradford has taken up the challenge by exploring spirituality within the context of care for the whole child. I hope that this book will be read carefully by those with responsibility for designing and delivering services to children and young people.

If we are to improve services for children, we must ensure that children's spiritual needs are addressed with the same concern as all other aspects of their well-being. If we want to keep the Nation's body and soul together we could do no better than start with the Nation's children.

JOHN BOWIS
Parliamentary Under Secretary of State
Department of Health

EDITORIAL PREFACE

Since the Children Act 1989 drew attention to the spiritual and religious needs of children it has generated discussion and debate about the inter-relationship between religious and 'professional' matters, not least in relation to day care provision. It has become clear, through discussions between Christian Child Care Network and the Department of Health, that further consideration of the nature and context of the spiritual and religious development of children and young people would be appreciated by all involved in child care. This includes central government and statutory authorities, voluntary child care organisations drawing their inspiration from the Christian faith, parents and schools, as well as Christian and other faith communities.

We turned to John Bradford, Chaplain Missioner to The Children's Society, because of his long interest and experience in this whole area. (I have known him since meeting at a seminar on the spiritual needs of children, held at Thomas Coram in The International Year of the Child in 1979.)

As the book has progressed from the germ of an idea to publication John has been assiduous in seeking comments and amending, developing and expanding the book in the light of recurring responses. John has been sensitive to the perspectives of different faith communities, and to the specific framework of both social services and educational law.

The subject is vast, and in some senses, infinite, so this is not a definitive textbook. However it is a valuable 'first' in this field and sets out a range of issues with clarity and coherence. The identification of spirituality with wholeness and the needs and aspirations of every child is timely, and the distinction between 'human' and 'devotional' spirituality helps to set religious faith and practice in context.

On behalf of all the agencies that comprise the UK CCCN I thank John for his labour of love, and The Children's Society for undertaking to publish the book for us all. It is our hope that it will be a resource not just to faith communities, but to all involved in the care, development and education of children. In particular we offer it to those seeking to implement the Children Act in whatever settings, whether by providing direct care, support and advice, management structures or registration and inspection.

Revd John Bradford is a practising Christian and this book is written by a committed person. Some might feel this would limit the book to those of a similar faith commitment. However, when using extracts from this book the reverse has, as CS Lewis anticipated, proved true: 'those at the heart of different faiths, including honest agnostics, find themselves closer together in understanding than those at the periphery of the same faith'.

If this work helps to develop our awareness of children as whole people and to give them, as Gibran advised so beautifully, 'our love not our thoughts', it will have amply served its purpose.

KEITH WHITE
Founder and Trustee
Christian Child Care Network
10 Crescent Road
South Woodford
London E18 1JB

Note:

Christian Child Care Network (CCCN) exists to link children and families in need with appropriate specialist Christian resources. Since its inception in 1990 it has responded to hundreds of requests for help from all over the UK. By 1995 it had over 850 resources on its database.

This direct daily contact with those in need has demonstrated the importance of careful conceptual work affecting policy and planning work. In 1994 CCCN hosted a conference of UK Christian Adoption Agencies. The launch of *Caring for the Whole Child* on 20 October 1995 will be, significantly, at a UK conference on 'counselling' of children in a Christian context. Such conferences are part of this process of reflecting on structural and societal issues in the light of the expressed cries for help of parents, families and counsellors.

INTRODUCTION

Caring for the whole child necessitates having a broad perspective on spirituality. Spirituality needs to be considered as a tripartite concept, the three parts of which — human, devotional and practical — fit closely together and complement the whole. It is a concept which is totally multicultural and multifaith in its applicability.

While the title of this book refers to caring for the whole 'child', it should be noted that by 'child' is meant a young person from infancy to the age of majority.

This book endeavours to show the potential of a tripartite understanding of spirituality both for social workers and educationalists. It is envisaged as a key resource to help these professionals examine their working principles in relation to how they regard their client or pupil as a person.

There is a corresponding hope that the Churches and other faith communities may become more thoughtfully supportive, not only to those in the human services professional sector who seek to promote the spirituality of the young in the broad and tripartite sense described, but particularly to the children and young people with whom these professionals work.

For half a century, following the Education Act 1944, local education authorities, Standing Advisory Councils on Religious Education, and teachers have been attentive to the notion of the spiritual development of pupils in school, and to the spiritual welfare of the community. However, generally speaking, only since the Children Act 1989 have social services departments and social workers been clearly constrained to be specifically attentive to the religious persuasion of children in care. *Caring for the Whole Child* provides a framework which is intended to enable those in both professions to think together about the personhood of the child in a new and constructive way.

At a time when the pressures of secularism and the fragmentation and dislocation of society are particularly pronounced, all those in human service organisations have a duty to review their presuppositions about spirituality. There is a very real need to work with children and young people in a way which promotes their overall well-being and development and which is inclusive of the 'devotional', or religious, dimension. It is hoped that the analysis offered will contribute to this process.

Key definitions

Spirituality	chapter 4, page 35
Spiritual needs	chapter 4, page 35
Spiritual development	section 4.5, page 40
Religious care	section 5.1, page 46
Principles of provision of religious care	section 5.5, page 51

1

THE HUMAN SPIRITUALITY

OF THE CHILD

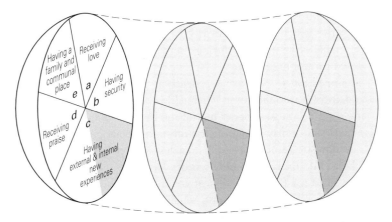

Figure 1 Human spirituality (about 'being')

Human spirituality describes the well-being and inter-relatedness of the emotional, cognitive and intuitive self, which includes sensitivity to the transcendent. It is developed through:

a love and affection;
b security;
c new experiences: (i) external, e.g. play and exploration; (ii) internal, e.g. opportunities for stillness, reflection, awe and wonder;
d praise and recognition;
e participation and responsibility.

1.1 Essential needs

The late Dr Mia Kellmer Pringle, the statement of principles of the National Council of Voluntary Child Care Organisations and the Barclay Report all speak in a way which suggests a common picture of the fundamental needs of children.[1, 2, 3]

Children may be said to have very particular needs in respect of the following five areas:

1. The need for the experience of a profound quality of *love*. This is usually from the child's natural parent(s). Love of this kind gives the child a sense of significance. A cuddle can communicate this meaningfully to the child.

2. The need for a sense of immediate and ultimate *security*. This refers both to a sense of 'being safe', and to a feeling of peace with the wider world. This may be emphasised for the child at moments of reassurance during the day, and when being settled down for the night.

3. The need for *new creative experiences* (i) in play and exploration, and also (ii) through some personal 'space' for the experience of inner peace and wonder. The linkage between these two realms of experience may sometimes be through the imagination, which can almost instantly be entered or left. For parents or carers to take a child on visits to new settings has value.

4. The need for the *affirmation* of others. Obviously there will be boundaries to be learnt about, which the child must keep within in order to enjoy praise and avoid blame. Being encouraged for positive behaviour, rather than admonished for negative, is fundamental to a sense of usefulness and 'direction'.

5. The need for the opportunity to *take part* in and contribute to the social well-being of their family and neighbourhood, and thus to experience a sense of community. Being involved, rather than left out or left behind, is important.

In simplified terms, these five categories refer to love, peace, wonder, confidence and relatedness.

Human spirituality is fundamentally about our identity as social beings, but assumes that the needs of our natural human identity – the needs of the body – are also being met. Bodily needs are by no means inessential, and can sometimes be the vehicle through which our human-spiritual needs are met.

Michael Ignatieff writes: [4]

> If you ask me what my needs are, I will tell you that I need the chance to understand and to be understood, to love and to be loved, to forgive and be forgiven, and the chance to create something that will outlast my life, and the chance to belong to a society whose purposes and commitments I share. But if you were to ask me what needs I have as a natural, as

opposed to a social being, I would quickly find myself restricted to those of my body.

1.2 Basic rights

What is particularly important to appreciate is that the human-spiritual needs of children, and the natural and appropriate fulfilment of those needs, should be recognised and supported by society. When parents, families and communities understand and accept this obligation then we are legitimately speaking of the human-spiritual *rights* of the child. Such children, when they become parents and adult family and community members, will then, in their turn, have responsibility for meeting those rights of children dependent on them.

The UN Convention on the Rights of the Child 1989, ratified by HM Government in December 1991, gives significant endorsement to such recognition.[5] Five key human-spiritual rights are identified below and these are supported by relevant extracts from the Convention.

1. **The right to the opportunity for a close and loving parental bond**

   Recognising that the child, for the full and harmonious development of his or her personality, should grow up in a family environment, in an atmosphere of happiness, love and understanding. [PREAMBLE, PARAGRAPH 6].

   States Parties shall respect the responsibilities, rights and duties of parents or, where applicable, the members of the extended family or community as provided for by the local custom, legal guardians or other persons legally responsible for the child, to provide, in a manner consistent with the evolving capacities of the child, appropriate direction and guidance in the exercise by the child of the rights recognized in the present Convention. [ARTICLE 5]

2. **The right to a cultural and physical environment which promotes a full sense of security**

   States Parties shall ensure that a child shall not be separated from his or her parents against their will, except when competent authorities subject to judicial review determine, in accordance with applicable law and procedures, that such separation is necessary for the best interests of the child. Such determination may be necessary in a particular case such as one involving abuse or neglect of the child by the parents, or one where the parents are living separately and a decision must be made as to the child's place of residence. [ARTICLE 9.1]

No child shall be subjected to arbitrary or unlawful interference with his or her privacy, family, home or correspondence, nor to unlawful attacks on his or her honour and reputation. [ARTICLE 16.1]

States Parties recognize the right of the child to be protected from economic exploitation and from performing any work that is likely to be hazardous or to interfere with the child's education, or to be harmful to the child's health or physical, mental, spiritual, moral or social development. [ARTICLE 32.1]

3. **The right to day–to–day circumstances (including mass media output) which allow the exercise of imagination, creativity, wonder and reflection**

The child shall have the right to freedom of expression; this right shall include freedom to seek, receive and impart information and ideas of all kinds, regardless of frontiers, either orally, in writing or in print, in the form of art, or through any other media of the child's choice. [ARTICLE 13.1]

States Parties recognize the important function performed by the mass media and shall ensure that the child has access to information and material from a diversity of national and international sources, especially those aimed at the promotion of his or her social, spiritual and moral well-being and physical and mental health. [ARTICLE 17]

States Parties recognize the right of the child to rest and leisure, to engage in play and recreational activities appropriate to the age of the child and to participate freely in cultural life and the arts.

States Parties shall respect and promote the right of the child to fully participate in cultural and artistic life and shall

encourage the provision of appropriate and equal opportunities for cultural, artistic, recreational and leisure activity.
[ARTICLE 31.1, 2]

4. **The right to a social context which is affirming and supportive**

States Parties recognize that a mentally or physically disabled child should enjoy a full and decent life, in conditions which ensure dignity, promote self-reliance, and facilitate the child's active participation in the community. [ARTICLE 23.1]

States Parties recognize the right of every child to a standard of living adequate for the child's physical, mental, moral and social development.

The parent(s) or others responsible for the child have the primary responsibility to secure, within their abilities and financial capacities, the conditions of living necessary for the child's development. [ARTICLE 27.1, 2]

5. **The right to age-appropriate inclusion as a participating member in family and community affairs**

States Parties agree that the education of the child shall be directed to:
(a) the development of the child's personality, talents and mental and physical abilities to their fullest potential;
(b) the development of respect for human rights and fundamental freedoms, and for the principles enshrined in the Charter of the United Nations;
(c) the development of respect for the child's parents, his or her own cultural identity, language and values, for the national values of the country in which the child is living, the country from which he or she may originate, and for civilizations different from his or her own;
(d) the preparation of the child for responsible life in a free society, in the spirit of understanding, peace, tolerance, equality of sexes, and friendship among all peoples, ethnic, national and religious groups and persons of indigenous origin;
(e) the development of respect for the natural environment.
[ARTICLE 29.1]

Summarised, these human spiritual rights are of:
1. love and affection;
2. security and serenity;
3. new experiences and wonder;
4. encouragement and support;
5. responsibility and participation.

1.3 Personal development

A child or young person develops in human spirituality and personal maturity if he or she:

1. has opportunity for loving and being loved, and of having within this experience the freedom for growth in individuality and personhood (as opposed to suffocation or over-protection);
2. has an increasing understanding and appreciation of creation and in particular of the value – and hope for – human life;
3. has moments of awareness and wonder, times when seemingly fragmented areas of knowledge and experience integrate to form a sound and cohesive whole, times when 'signs of transcendence' are seen in such experiences as play, hope, outrage and humour (Berger) [6] and space for reflection upon such instances;
4. has a desire to create or contribute something that will outlast his or her life, and has perseverance in pursuing goodness, beauty and truth;
5. has the chance to identify with, and to thrive within, a family or community whose values and commitments he or she shares, and whose resolve to resist those things which corrode, compromise or corrupt is similarly accepted.

It has been usefully observed by Rabbi Jonathan Sacks that: [7]

> The family is not one social institution among others, nor is it simply one lifestyle choice among many. It is the best means we have yet discovered for nurturing future generations, and for enabling children to grow in a matrix of stability and love. It is where we acquire the skills and language of relationship. It is where we learn to handle the inevitable conflicts within any human group. It is where we first take the risk of giving and receiving love. Of all the influences upon us, the family is by far the most powerful. Its effects stay with us for a lifetime.

[Handwritten margin notes: "all 3", "Spiritual within environments", "All necessary & found & environments", "relationship with staff", "would be school?", "safe place", "Have friends", "best place", "Next", "↳ what if the family isn't empowering?"]

It is where one generation passes on its values to the next and ensures the continuity of a civilisation. Nothing else – not teachers or schools, not politicians or the media – so shapes us and what we have a chance of becoming as our experience of early childhood. For any society, the family is the crucible of its future.

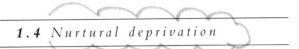

1.4 Nurtural deprivation

Unfortunately some children do not receive full and caring support for the development of their human spirituality. In certain cases, but not all, this may be the result of hardship or disadvantage suffered by the parent or parents. Nurtural deprivation in a child's human spirituality may take the following forms (though the list is not exhaustive):

1. parental coolness and distancing from the child;
2. parental separation, the absence of one parent and the possible disruption and uncertainty (actual or envisaged) in adult caring which these circumstances can give rise to – for example the possibility of living, not simply with a step-parent, but with a step-family and the sibling rivalries which that could entail;
3. social and environmental deprivation – having a parent or parents who are unemployed and living on benefit and the restrictions and resentments which this can give rise to, or of living in substandard housing and/or in areas of social priority with a lack of aesthetically pleasing surroundings or safe and spacious play opportunities;
4. suffering, or having a parent or close relative or friend, suffer sudden loss, illness or mishap with no pattern for coping or length of time for understanding and adjustment;
5. being ignored, or made to feel irrelevant, at home, at school or in the neighbourhood or being made to feel a sense of worthlessness, which may inhibit or distort a capacity for forming social relationships.

Human-spiritual deprivation is therefore suffered when a child or young person does not receive sufficient stimulation to be touched by:

1. being loved, including awareness that those closest and dearest have one's best interests at heart, both in the short and long term;

2. a sense of belonging and of having an intuition of immediate and ultimate security, no matter how adverse circumstances may be;

3. moments of being 'called out beyond oneself', for example in awe at an insight into the harmony and beauty of nature, in humour, in reacting to injustice, in having hope, and in being able to enter imaginatively into a game;

4. a consciousness of the affirmation of others, especially when acting with human spirituality, i.e. when reciprocating love, showing trust, being creative, giving encouragement and thinking of others;

5. the expectation and welcome in having a place in contributing to the shared activities of family and community.

In the light of this, it may be appreciated that for some young people to run away from home or from care is a human-spiritual experience. They run to where they find comradeship, they discover streetwise knowledge of the 'safe' places to sleep, they take a step of hope of there being something better than their present situation at home or in care, they have the encouragement of at least some of their fellow street youth, and they feel part of a particular sub-culture and sub-community. Any work in bringing young people out of such a highly risk-ridden lifestyle should not detract from a recognition of some of the human-spiritual positives in their having taken that option in the first place.

1.5 Nurtural damage

Human-spiritual support for a child may sometimes not merely be inadequate, but may be of a fractured, perverse or even malevolent nature so that an injurious experience takes the place of what should have been a benign and beneficial one. Human-spiritual damage is likely to have occurred if a child:

1. has had nurture experiences of intentional injury, neglect or abuse. Jean-Pierre Kirkland helps us to see the value in supporting the spiritual needs of such children. Kirkland recognises that in school the abused child is likely to be under far more stress than the rest of the class. He advocates an approach which makes provision for such children to have space to relax, calm to focus the mind through the use of certain meditative techniques, and opportunity for shared reflection about experiences and feelings.[8]

2. has had very disruptive changes in home circumstances and extremely sudden and distressing alterations in care arrangements, with no opportunity for preparation or adjustment. Melanie Phillips, a journalist, makes a point about the effects of family breakdown in a strikingly forthright way, even if in many cases her remarks might be considered more relevant to human-spiritual deprivation rather than damage: [9]

> To prevent such damage from being inflicted, our culture has to change so that fragmented families, transient affairs and serial relationships are no longer promoted as admirable but are presented more realistically as disastrous for the children and therefore to be avoided wherever possible. That would not mean that parents had to stay together, however dreadful their marriage; but it would mean that people were no longer able to kid themselves that dissolving and reforming their families was free of harmful consequences.

3. has been nurtured by those with attitudes of marked bigotry, fitful oppression or general confusion and has had to recourse to fearful withdrawal rather than to inner stillness;
4. has been exposed to predominantly punitive, chaotic, inconsistent or demeaning child-rearing patterns;
5. has been unreasonably denied or excluded from family or community gatherings, or inappropriately included in aberrant family and community acts (e.g. verbal abuse, violence or vandalism).

Damage may take many years to heal or to come to terms with. The caring ministry and understanding of a person's faith community may be one form of therapeutic support (see section 7.4 on pages 68–70), and in schools the pastoral provision may be significant. In adulthood the healing aspect of marriage may well be of great benefit over time, as Dr Jack Dominian points out.[10]

However, it is important to see ourselves and each other through a realistic and optimistic lens. The following insight from Metropolitan Anthony Bloom, from a Christian perspective, may be helpful: [11]

> Unless we look at a person and see the beauty there is in this person, we cannot contribute anything to him. One does not help a person by discerning what is wrong, what is ugly, what is distorted. Christ looked at everyone He met, at the

prostitute, at the thief and saw the beauty hidden there. Perhaps it was distorted, perhaps damaged, but it was beauty nonetheless, and what He did was call out to this beauty... This is what we must learn to do with regard to others. But to do so we must first have a purity of heart, a purity of intention, an openness which is not always there... so that we can listen, can look, and can see the beauty which is hidden. Every one of us is in the image of God, and every one of us is like a damaged icon. But if we were given an icon damaged by time, damaged by circumstances, or desecrated by human hatred, we would treat it with reverence, with tenderness, with broken-heartedness. We would not pay attention primarily to the fact that it is damaged, but to the tragedy of its being damaged. We would concentrate on what is left of its beauty and not on what is lost of its beauty. And this is what we must learn to do with regard to each person.

2

THE DEVOTIONAL SPIRITUALITY

OF THE CHILD

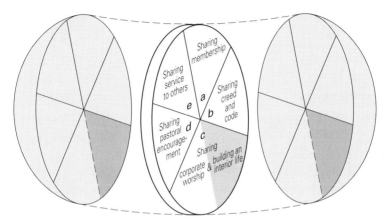

Figure 2 Devotional spirituality (about 'belonging')

Devotional spirituality refers to the formation of a corporate and personal religious life.

The pursuit of devotional spirituality – the practised affiliation to a particular religion – will offer:

a religious identity and warmth of membership;

b security of established creed and moral code;

c possibilities for growth and discovery through (i) corporate worship and scriptural tradition; (ii) the formation of a distinctive personal and inner devotional life;

d support of pastoral encouragement and the intercession of others;

e multiple opportunities for taking part within the local faith community, and for 'serving', or helping and having concern for others.

2.1 *Distinctive needs*

It is essential to see religion – devotional spirituality – as giving order to, articulating and endorsing human spirituality.

Human spirituality		Devotional spirituality
being loved	*becomes*	having identity as a member
feeling secure	*becomes*	being nurtured in sound tradition
responding in wonder	*becomes*	having a framework for worship and a focus for contemplation
being affirmed	*becomes*	being empowered to affirm others and to share peace or 'shalom'
sharing together	*becomes*	participation in community

The factors listed as devotional spirituality are fundamental to religious identity of all kinds. They apply equally, for example, to a Muslim as to a member of the Society of Friends.

The process by which devotional spirituality builds upon and transmutes experience from human spirituality is profound. As F Brabant has observed: [12]

> Now Professor Otto is perfectly right in maintaining (and it is the important teaching of his great work) that the process by which this wonder becomes religious is unique; the sense of fear and astonishment before the greatness and strangeness of the universe is not yet religious; it needs the direct and irreducible experience of personal relationship to become worship.

Under certain circumstances human-spiritual needs and devotional-spiritual needs may be seen to be indistinguishable. However, this is not to say that they are the same. Every child may be said to have human-spiritual needs, whether they have a religion or not, and an unhealthy or isolationist religion (see section 7.5, page 71) may be shown not to coalesce well with a child's human-spiritual needs.

The technical difference is that all children, young people and adults should be seen as having human-spiritual needs. What we call devotional-spiritual needs will be human-spiritual needs expressed in the culture and language of a particular religion and which enhance attunement to the Divine. A religion makes the invaluable contribution of providing a language, culture and tradition within which the significance of personal and ultimate issues (e.g. the purpose of life) can be articulated, shared and reflected upon.

This is not to assert that all religious cultures are the same but that human-spiritual factors require the thought-forms and belief-system of a particular religion in order to have added value in depth, coherence and attunement to the transcendent. It is therefore helpful to see involvement in a particular religion as being functional in giving a distinctive framework, context and language to a child who might otherwise be experiencing sporadic moments of spiritual attunement such as experiences of awe and wonder, or of transcendental love and acceptance.

The distinctive insights and approach of each major world religion may be seen to prioritise and enhance human-spiritual factors in a slightly different way. For example, Christianity may be seen to have a special link with love and forgiveness, Islam with wonder, Buddhism with inner serenity, Hinduism with affirmation, and Confucianism and Shintoism with a sense of relatedness. These links are only suggestions for the sake of argument; each religion will have affinity with all human-spiritual fields but nevertheless will weigh these differently according to their own insights and doctrines.

Since young people are intrinsically curious and prone to boundary testing it is therefore important to make a firm distinction between a tripartite understanding of spirituality, of which devotional spirituality is a core section, and the occult and certain 'New Age' understandings of spirituality. The latter are seen as an aberration of the spiritual and as being no part of mainstream devotional spirituality whatsoever.

Where the characteristics of devotional spirituality may be seen to be (i) membership; (ii) sound tradition; (iii) worship and contemplation; (iv) affirming others; and (v) community concern, the characteristics of the occult are the very antithesis of these.

Participation in the occult will involve (i) de-personalisation from being an individual into being a 'player'; (ii) valuing irrationality and instant experiences of the mysterious; (iii) being totally open to and influenced by a completely unknown 'force'; (iv) being primarily interested in one's own fate or fortune; and (v) being vulnerable to the manipulation of the untested beliefs of others, and to possibly becoming, in turn, similarly manipulative.

Membership of a main world religion involves commitment for life; involvement in the occult could be a single one-off experience such as taking part in a seance. However, the risk of personal disturbance and inner dissatisfaction may be considerable.

2.2 Particular rights

The use of the concept of religious 'rights' is an especially positive tool in a multifaith society for supporting the devotional spirituality of the young.

Having noted the spiritually integrative function of a main world religion, let us identify the religious rights of the child as these are contained in the UN Convention on the Rights of the Child 1989.

1. **The right of the child or young person to be nurtured in their parents' religious beliefs**. This right is limited by the provision in Article 5 dealing with the rights and responsibilities of parents, family and community, where it is said that this shall be in a manner consistent with the evolving capacities of the child.

   States Parties shall respect the right of the child to freedom of thought, conscience and religion. [ARTICLE 14.1]

   States Parties shall respect the rights and duties of the parents and, when applicable, legal guardians, to provide direction to the child in the exercise of his or her right in a manner consistent with the evolving capacities of the child. [ARTICLE 14.2]

   States Parties shall respect the responsibilities, rights and duties of parents or, where applicable, the members of the extended family or community as provided for by local custom, legal guardians or other persons legally responsible for the child, to provide, in a manner consistent with the evolving capacities of the child, appropriate direction and guidance in the exercise by the child of the rights recognized in the present Convention. [ARTICLE 5]

2. **The right of the child or young person to express (manifest) their religion or belief**, which implies freedom also to regulate their behaviour in the light of this, for example in food, dress and religious observance.

   Freedom to manifest one's religion or beliefs may be subject only to such limitations as are prescribed by law and are necessary to protect public safety, order, health or morals, or the fundamental rights and freedoms of others. [ARTICLE 14.3]

In those States in which ethnic, religious or linguistic minorities or persons of indigenous origin exist, a child belonging to such a minority or who is indigenous shall not be denied the right, in community with other members of his or her group, to enjoy his or her own culture, to profess and practise his or her own religion, or to use his or her own language.
[ARTICLE 30]

3. **The right of the child to freedom of thought, conscience and religion** as provided for adults in the 1948 Universal Declaration of Human Rights. This right to belief, while not explicitly providing for a child or young person to have the freedom to adopt a religion or belief (other than that of their parents), nevertheless is to be interpreted in the light of Article 12 (on the free expression of opinion).

This freedom of devotional spirituality also refers to the informed choice of a child or adult to practise, deepen or develop his or her religious devotional life in a particular way. This will probably include a combination of acts of devotion in common with others of the same faith community, together with a rule or pattern for private and personal study, prayer and meditation, and social concern.

States Parties shall respect the right of the child to freedom of thought, conscience and religion. [ARTICLE 14.1]

States Parties shall assure to the child who is capable of forming his or her own views the right to express those views freely in all matters affecting the child, the views of the child being given due weight in accordance with the age and maturity of the child. [ARTICLE 12.10]

4. **The right of the child or young person to familial, educational and social respect, and *support* for their religious identity and values**

Recognizing that the United Nations has, in the Universal Declaration of Human Rights and in the International Covenants on Human Rights, proclaimed and agreed that everyone is entitled to all the rights and freedoms set forth therein, without distinction of any kind, such as race, colour, sex, language, religion, political or other opinion, national or social origin, property, birth or other status, in suitable institutions for the care of children. When considering solutions, due regard shall be paid to the desirability of continuity in a child's upbringing and to the child's ethnic, religious, cultural and linguistic background. [PREAMBLE, PARAGRAPH 3]

1. A child temporarily or permanently deprived of his or her family environment, or in whose own best interests cannot be allowed to remain in that environment, shall be entitled to special protection and assistance provided by the State.

2. States Parties shall, in accordance with their national laws, ensure alternative care for such a child.

3. Such care could include, *inter alia*, foster placement, *kafalah* of Islamic law, adoption or, if necessary, placement in suitable institutions for the care of children. When considering solutions, due regard shall be paid to the desirability of continuity in a child's upbringing and to the child's ethnic, religious, cultural and linguistic background. [ARTICLE 20]

c) The development of respect for the child's parents, his or her own cultural identity, language and values, for the national values of the country in which the child is living, the country from which he or she may originate, and for civilizations different from his or her own; [ARTICLE 29]

In those states in which ethnic, religious or linguistic minorities or persons of indigenous origin exist, a child belonging to such a minority or who is indigenous shall not be denied the right, in community with other members of his or her group, to enjoy his or her own culture, to profess and practise his or her own religion, or to use his or her own language. [ARTICLE 30]

5. **The right of the child or young person to protection from religious discrimination, to education for religious tolerance and for friendship among all peoples**. This may be associated also with the right to protection from sexual exploitation (Article 34) or degrading punishment or deprivation of liberty (Article 37 (a) and (b)).

1. States Parties shall respect and ensure the rights set forth in the present Convention to each child within their jurisdiction without discrimination of any kind, irrespective of the child's or his or her parent's or legal guardian's race, colour, sex,

language, religion, political or other opinion, national, ethnic or social origin, property, disability, birth or other status.

2. States Parties shall take all appropriate measures to ensure that the child is protected against all forms of discrimination or punishment on the basis of the status, activities, expressed opinions, or beliefs of the child's parents, legal guardians, or family members. [ARTICLE 2]

(d) The preparation of the child for responsible life in a free society, in the spirit of understanding, peace, tolerance, equality of sexes, and friendship among all peoples, ethnic, national and religious groups and persons of indigenous origin; [ARTICLE 29]

Children and young people should receive help and support from faith communities, particularly in respect of some more general rights of protection.

States Parties undertake to protect the child from all forms of sexual exploitation and sexual abuse. For these purposes, States Parties shall in particular take all appropriate national, bilateral and multilateral measures to prevent:
(a) The inducement or coercion of a child to engage in any unlawful sexual activity;
(b) The exploitative use of children in prostitution or other unlawful sexual practices;
(c) The exploitative use of children in pornographic performances and materials. [ARTICLE 34]

States Parties shall ensure that:
(a) No child shall be subjected to torture or other cruel, inhuman or degrading treatment or punishment. Neither capital punishment nor life imprisonment without possibility of release shall be imposed for offenses committed by persons below eighteen years of age;
(b) No child shall be deprived of his or her liberty unlawfully or arbitrarily. The arrest, detention or imprisonment of a child shall be in conformity with the law and shall be used only as a measure of last resort and for the shortest appropriate period of time; [ARTICLE 37]

Thus the five devotional-spiritual rights of the child or young person may be summarised as:

1. nurture;
2. expression;
3. choice (e.g. to deepen or doubt);
4. support;
5. protection.

2.3 Faith community integration

Membership of a faith community can undoubtedly help a child in his or her overall devotional-spiritual development by providing a framework of a common code, creed, and pattern of worship and fellowship which values and gives space to spiritual experience. This frees the child from remaining unaware of, or from suppressing, the human-spiritual experiences they may be having.

More particularly, membership of a healthy faith community should:

1. offer a network of benevolent and respectful relationships – a community of friends;
2. offer membership in a community which has a sense of awareness about its place in the wider scheme of things;
3. offer an involvement with others who are reverently and thoughtfully open to signs of Providence in day-to-day experience, and who are supportive of the internalisation and ongoing meditation about them;
4. offer participation in a community which is mutually affirming in experiencing the qualities of love, trust, wonder, and so on;
5. offer roles for contributing to shared cultural and other actions which express the values of the community.

Such religious involvement should strengthen a child's resilience to difficulty or misadventure of all kinds (see section 3.2 on pages 27–29). Judith Allen Shelly et al., writing from a Christian perspective, indicate how valuable such faith support can be to ill or dying children.[13]

The religious scenario depicted above is intended to reflect the strengths of a good and positive example of a local faith community of any main world faith.

A child requires affiliation to a particular religion/denomination according to his culture and background. He or she cannot relate to, or receive benefit from, 'religions in general.' His or her parental religious affiliation is part of his or her own identity. (Learning about other belief systems is, of course, a different matter.)

The thinking of John H Westerhoff III is particularly valuable in considering the faith development of children and young people, which he sees as passing through an 'Experienced Faith Process' (early childhood), an 'Affiliative Faith Process' (primary/middle years), a 'Searching Faith Process' (adolescence) and a 'Mature Faith Process' (adulthood).[14]

'Experienced faith' refers to the stage where the faith demonstrated by an infant's parents, family and friends is unconsciously copied. 'Affiliative faith' refers to sharing faith expression naturally with others, especially of one's age group, for example in a congregation or religious camp. 'Searching faith' refers to the questioning developmental stage of the teenager and young adult, when all accepted norms are challenged, and 'mature faith' refers to when the faith previously shown, shared and questioned is finally 'owned' (i.e. consciously accepted and, if appropriate, openly acknowledged).

In Westerhoff's view, as we grow outwards in faith – rather like rings on a tree – we do not simply leave one style of faith behind and attain a new style, but rather each new style is added on to the previous ones. (Note Westerhoff's use of the term 'style' rather than 'stage'.) This analogy makes it clear that to have missed the experiential and affiliative processes in our early years is a loss which may have to be made up in later life. We can only progress when the needs of an earlier style of faith have been satisfied.

A diagram of Westerhoff's tree-trunk analogy may be helpful:

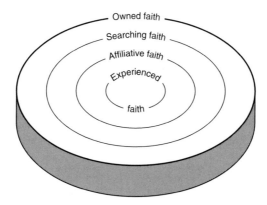

Owned faith

Searching faith

Affiliative faith

Experienced

faith

Source: *How Faith Grows* [15]

Figure 3 Westerhoff's tree-trunk analogy

Westerhoff says: [16]

> For many adolescents, even those brought up in the Church, the experience of loneliness, self-hatred, family conflict, estrangement, insecurity, closed-mindedness, dogmatic author- ity, and an affectionless environment have made searching faith difficult to attain. In spite of their adolescent social condi- tion, they need a community which nurtures affiliative faith.

In Westerhoff's view, a healthy faith community should act as a bridge over the troubled water of a difficult home or a difficult adolescence.

2.4 Devotional-spiritual deprivation

Children and young people may come from homes and neighbour- hoods or backgrounds where the foundations of devotional-spiritu- ality have been absent, or presented or referred to only in a distort- ing way. As a result some children and young people:

1. may have had little or no religious nurture and may only possess some disjointed, superficial knowledge – possibly blurring the boundaries of the main world faiths;
2. may find themselves wishing to express what faith they have in somewhat bizarre or anti-social ways;
3. may not be consciously open to religious growth or develop- ment, but may prefer to take refuge in prejudiced opinion;
4. may present a problem to those wishing to respect their religious tradition and values since these may not correlate with any degree of significance to a particular world faith;
5. may have been exposed to attitudes of discrimination, intolerance and disrespect.

A central paradox of the human condition in urbanised societies is that those who most need the security, reassurance and supportive frame- work of religion both for their personal and social development – i.e. those who are subject to marked difficulty, isolation, alienation, disad- vantage or stress – are all too often those without any religion at all.

Some might have little more than a favourite religious building or location (which could be a cemetery), a favourite song, story or phrase, or a favourite religious picture, medallion or other artefact. These would have a value to the holder out of all proportion to normal expectation, as in the story behind Gavin Bryars' song

'Jesus' Blood Never Failed Me Yet', which was the single refrain sung by a tramp over and over again in great sincerity and to his personal comfort.[17]

Furthermore, for the chaos and pain of traumatic human experience to be safely expressed, it must be contained rather than allowed to be expressed destructively or uncontrollably. A religion provides the great stories and images for such expression and containment to take place.

Although one of the aims of the psychoanalyst is to safely contain the expression of chaos and pain of the human experience, not every child will receive the benefit of an analysis at this depth. However, much of an individual's chaos and pain can be better understood and contained when that individual can identify with the great stories and images in the world religions. Once the individual knows where he or she can find such relief, there is a never-ending source of expression and containment (Bion).[18]

Margaret Crompton gives concrete examples of a similar type of approach in counselling. She outlines, for example, the uses of music, artwork and story within counselling sessions.[19] Carefully prepared and presented, this approach could be amalgamated with the use of the great stories and images of the world religions in analysis, to positive effect.

2.5 Institutional damage

It should be noted that religions are human institutions liable to error and that, at worst, religious institutions themselves can de-spiritualise in the sense of working against human spirituality.

It is therefore not sufficient to speak only of religious rights or duties because, in the case of bizarre and unhealthy cults and groups, the religious may impair or obliterate the human-spiritual. Where human-spiritual rights and devotional-spiritual religious rights are in conflict, it is the former which should generally be regarded as primary.

Satanism may be seen as an extreme but clear example of where the 'religious' impairs or obliterates the human-spiritual. The oppressive circumstances for children of Jonestown, Guyana, of the community of David Koresh in Texas, and of the Solar Disc cult of Switzerland and Canada would hardly have continued if the human-spiritual needs and rights of the child had been seen to be primary. The tragic massacre of children in the holocaust was a denial of their human spirituality, their devotional-spiritual rights and their practical spirituality.

A measure of de-spiritualisation can also take place at ordinary levels of faith community life where relationships are uncaring and examples set by senior members are negative. This must never be condoned.

It should be noted that child abuse by a religious professional is a most profoundly damaging phenomenon. Thankfully, religious communities are becoming more attentive to this risk. Along with parental abuse, abuse by a leader or member of a local faith community can shatter and undermine a young person's sense of self-worth, capacity for trust and sense of the sacred.

However, rather than compounding difficulties, and in order to accept and affirm those with only the barest fragment of devotional spirituality, a faith community should be encouraged to:

1. see that it is open to endorse the rites of passage of those who may not formally fall within its membership;
2. offer a form of celebration at Great Festivals, or other appropriate occasions, when the faith community can give recognition and hospitality to those who would wish to be associated, even though in a fragmented way;
3. receive reports from, and have devotional concern for, those working with the disadvantaged;
4. encourage religious communities to have a special concern for the human spirituality of those without religious affiliation and to intercede on their behalf;
5. be constructively responsive to the needs of children, young people and their families who are of mixed denomination or faith;
6. have systems for ensuring that those working with children and young people are suitably qualified and of personal integrity such as, for example, recent guidelines by the Diocese of Lichfield.[20]

A faith community should always be seeking to edify and encourage its members, especially younger ones, and to gently lead them on to a deeper understanding of truth, and a fuller and perhaps more appropriate use of their personal gifts, in harmony with other members. Faith communities should not make someone with little or no religious background feel insignificant or an 'outsider'. Rather, they might seek to discover such an individual's 'philosophy of life' and encourage them to pursue an existing interest, in their own time, which correlates with the beliefs and concerns of the faith community and which forms an authentic connecting point.

3

THE PRACTICAL SPIRITUALITY

OF THE CHILD

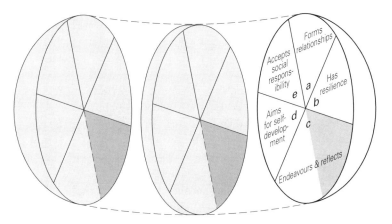

Figure 4 Practical spirituality (about 'acting')

Practical spirituality describes signs of the integration of human and devotional spirituality in everyday living. It refers to the vital principles, frame of mind and activating emotions of a person as they engage and participate in life. It is realised through:

a a capacity for affection, friendship and humanity of interaction;

b a capacity for resilience – coping constructively with difficulty and dissonance;

c a capacity for both (i) endeavour and enquiry; (ii) reverence and reflection;

d a capacity for confidence in being open to growth and self-developme̶n̶t̶ ̶a̶n̶d̶ in promoting the development of others;

e a capacit̶y̶ ̶f̶o̶r̶ ̶a̶p̶preciation of community, and for a sense of interpe̶r̶s̶o̶n̶a̶l̶ social responsibility.

The follow̶i̶n̶g̶ ̶q̶uotation by HRH The Prince of Wales provides a useful analog̶y̶ for thinking about practical spirituality: [21]

'The city is the image of the soul,' wrote Catherine of Siena, 'the surrounding walls being the frontier between the outward and the inward life. The gates are the faculties or senses connecting the life of the soul with the outward world. Living springs of water rise within it. And in the centre, where beats the heart, stands the holy sanctuary.'

3.1 Friendship

A person who has had a loving parental (or surrogate parental) background and a warm experience of faith community member-ship is well-equipped for affection, friendship and humanity of interaction in their own lives.

The building of friendships necessarily includes respect for, interest in and reciprocity of many aspects of each other's spiritu-ality – human, devotional and practical. Friendships may be more individually-based or – as Jean Vanier has pioneered in his l'Arche communities for the able-bodied and those with disabili-ties living together – community-based.[22]

Having humane relationships with others is not simply a matter of reducing vandalism on an estate (important though that is). Our living in society at large, and in the world community of some five or six billion others, demands of us either a negative reaction to our neighbour as one with whom we compete or whom we merely observe, ignore or even reject; or a positive reaction, as one whom we befriend, enable and help. It is no light matter that the future of world society lies at the heart of our spiritual attitude, displayed in our practical spirituality, towards our fellow human beings whom we do not know but with whom we share a common humanity. Our devotional spirituality (especially in the sense of our being loved by the Divine) can be of powerful assistance to us in this con-nection, as in others.

Affection and friendship involve meeting the reality of the other person. To be present with another is to allow their otherness to challenge and confront us, thereby changing our perception of their reality and of our own. As Rabbi Jonathan Sacks has said: [23]

> I believe that our capacity to recognise the 'wholly Other' that is God is measured by our ability to recognise the image of God that resides in the person who is not like us: the human 'wholly other.' The Bible commands us only once to love our neighbour. But it never tires of urging us to love the stranger. To have faith in God as creator and ruler of the universe is to do more than to

believe that God has spoken to us. It is to believe that God has spoken to others, in a language which we may not understand. After Babel, there is no one universal language which alone comprehends God, such that those who do not speak it are excluded from salvation, redemption or truth. Until that proposition frames our religious imagination, our faiths will contain devastating possibilities.

3.2 Resilience

Practical spirituality involves a capacity for coping constructively with difficulty and dissonance.

Resilience may be said to be the capacity of a human being to endure hardship and recover with maturity and wisdom to lead a meaningful and productive life. Both the human-spiritual qualities of a child, young person or adult, and their religious beliefs and associations can be seen to help provide them with resilience.

However, worship should, above all, be the acknowledgement of the 'worth' of the Divine. A religion should not be espoused and devotional spirituality should not be pursued with the sole intention of having a personal anchor in times of difficulty, but a religious commitment can provide the following as a by-product:

1. a pre-hardship network of care and understanding;
2. an in-crisis mode of safety and survival;
3. a post-hardship framework for interpretation and rehabilitation.

In this connection we should note the importance of young people discovering meaning in their lives. In *Life and How to Survive It* by Robin Skynner and John Cleese, three factors are pinpointed which help families cope with stressful changes: (i) rest; (ii) advice and information from people in similar circumstances; and (iii) emotional support from the family and community, and a transcendent value system. The transcendent value system refers to a 'set of values and beliefs which gives a sense of meaning and purpose going beyond their [those who are suffering] own welfare. The greatest source of value came from something much larger than themselves, beyond their family, something which provided a feeling of meaning and purpose which could survive loss and change of all kinds'.[24]

Some children and young people face circumstances of considerable pain and disruption. The place of a belief system and faith community involvement in offering some comfort and stability should not be disregarded.

It may be useful to consider that an appreciation of the Divine can give a sense of happiness and satisfaction in the journey of life. The example of an ordinary journey from A to B can be illustrative. If we are looking forward to what lies ahead at the end of our journey, the whole process of travel will take on a positive and acceptable tone. We will take a book or magazine to read, feel well disposed towards our travelling companions, enjoy the scenery and so on. If, however, we are not sure where we are going, or worse, have anxiety about its pointless or unpleasant end, then our attitude towards the process of travel – the journey itself – will be necessarily prejudiced and will almost certainly be negative.

As the Tavistock Institute of Marital Studies has observed, faith communities 'are communities in which significant life events are marked, celebrated, ritualised and endowed with symbolism. This is particularly helpful in assisting people to manage changes in their lives, providing as it does community recognition and support for the people concerned, and a framework within which individual meanings can be fashioned.' [25]

The following list from a newsletter produced by the International Catholic Child Bureau, New York, may be helpful in considering resilience. [26]

Protective factors which can bolster resilience:

● stable emotional relationships with at least one parent or other caregiver;

● social supports from inside and outside the family: relatives, neighbors, teachers, peers, clergy;

● an emotionally positive, open, guiding, and norm-oriented educational climate;

● social models that encourage constructive coping (e.g. parents, siblings, teachers, friends);

● balance of social responsibilities and achievement demands (e.g. care for relatives, at school);

● cognitive competence (e.g. an at least average level of intelligence, communication skills, empathy, realistic planning);

- temperament characteristics that favor effective coping *(e.g. flexibility, approach orientation, reflection and impulse control, strong interpersonal skills, good verbal communication skills);*

- experiences of self-efficacy, internal locus of control, corresponding self-confidence, and a positive self-concept;

- the way in which the individual deals with stressors, particularly by actively trying to cope;

- the experience of sense, structure, and meaning in one's own development *(e.g. faith, religion, ideology, sense of coherence).*

A most valuable resource for studying further the topic of resilience is the paper by Stefan Vanistendael, *Growth in the Muddle of Life: Resilience – Building on People's Strengths.*[27]

3.3 *Endeavour and reflection*

Practical spirituality includes an outworking of a capacity for both endeavour and enterprise, and for reflection and reverence (Lamb).[28]

As John H Westerhoff III says:[29]

> Faith, as I have used the word, is a verb. Faith is a way of behaving which involves knowing, being, and willing. The content of faith is best described in terms of our world-view and value system, but faith itself is something we do. Faith is an action. It results from our actions with others, it changes and expands through our actions with others, and it expresses itself daily in our actions with others.

Our profile of practical spirituality, therefore, describes the activities of an individual's personal life in which he or she consciously or unconsciously draws upon both his or her own human–spiritual and devotional-spiritual insights, experiences and resources. The emerging development of a personal profile of practical spirituality marked by goodwill and generosity is more difficult for someone who is deprived or damaged in human spirituality, and for those who do not wish to explore devotional spirituality, because their world-view and value system (see section 4.1 on pages 35–36) is likely to be constricted.

Broadly speaking, a profile of practical spirituality marked by goodwill and generosity refers to someone whose devotional spirituality has led them to a predominant disposition of one, or some combination, of the following.

Approaching 'endeavour' (c) as a way of:
- serving others
- using our skills
- contributing to progress
- being creative
- being constructively collaborative
- obtaining a usefully productive surplus
- supporting one's dependents
- conserving the environment
- glorifying God

Each of these dispositions will have impact on a person's lived-out, or practical, spirituality. It will be seen that some positions are more individualistic than others, some more corporate. A profile of practical spirituality which is balanced and robust will blend some characteristics of 'activism' with some of 'inner renewal'.

'Endeavour' may or may not be correlated with employment. For children and young people endeavour will clearly not mean 'gainful employment' but rather a purposeful use of time.

Unfortunately, the disproportionately large amount of time spent by many in watching the media or in playing computer games is, in general, a passive and non-purposeful use of time and may often be a substitute for quality parental conversation and attention time.

'Reflection' is the partner experience to endeavour in any balanced and considered lifestyle. Practical spirituality necessitates a reflecting process as the corollary of endeavour. Reflection will include consideration about why we do what we do, the way it fits in with our perceptions of how the world should be, and the way it flows from and expresses our beliefs and values – or challenges these.

Such reflection may occur, regularly or periodically, in private thought or private prayer, in a discussion group (e.g. of a school or college, trade or professional association, political conference) or on a religious retreat or pilgrimage. In reading, biography may be of particular value since it should be a portrayal of the subject's practical spirituality, from which lessons may be gained.

3.4 Growth and development

Those who have had praise and encouragement in the home and faith community should feel confident and have sound self-esteem in developing their potential and in exploring God's world and its opportunities. Such a person should feel that they wish to encourage others in their growth and exploration in life, and to be suitably in control of their relationships and general situation.

It is suggested that in the tradition of the monotheistic religions, finding – or being found by – God should be seen as being possible for anyone, at any age or stage of development, if they are prepared to dig deep enough into their own lives and situations and thus find 'evidence' of God's hand already at work. This will not necessarily mean the discovery of Divine 'power' in a fairly obvious and dramatic sense, but rather some indication of 'presence', 'providence' or the sense of the companionship of a 'hidden friend'. Such an experience is always open to anyone at any stage in their path through life. It will be complementary to, influential upon and integrative to their existing human and practical spirituality.

In the spirit of the thinking of Carl Jung, a religious outlook is a key factor in a positive attitude to life and in the opportunities for personal growth and development which it provides.[30] Devotional spirituality can give a sense of vivacity to our lived-out, or practical, spirituality.

Christopher Bryant gives a useful recommendation about spiritual reading, which could apply to those of any main world religion: [31]

> The ancient practice of *lectio divina*, spiritual reading, can be made a valuable instrument for involving the whole personality in responding to God. This reading, quite unlike most secular reading, is, properly understood, a kind of meditation, a means of communing both with God and with one's own depths. It is, I think, important that we should use this reading to develop, if we can, our weaker or less developed functions. Thus, if I am a thinker I must do what I can to allow my feelings to be roused, to express judgements of value, of right and wrong. If I am of feeling type I must not skate over a thought-provoking passage but must make myself reflect on it, perhaps by writing down some comment on it or summary of the argument. One should pause over a passage that strikes home and causes reverber-

ations deep within and not resume reading until the words or ideas have made their full impact.

3.5 Social responsibility

It must be emphasised that the human spirituality and the practised religion or devotional spirituality of anyone must be seen to lack integrity if these do not come to involve, or be accompanied by, a civic sense and by an active concern for those who experience poverty or disadvantage in the neighbourhood, the nation and the world.

Clearly this will be a challenge to personal acts of care, kindness, neighbourliness, service and participation of different kinds. Active concern for these people is by no means the preserve of the affluent for the non-affluent, but rather part of a concern of all for the common good.

Social responsibility will also include a concern for the environment, not least as a common heritage which it is our duty to pass on to future generations in as well-preserved and unpolluted a state as possible.

The practice of social responsibility will tend to bring the individual into solidarity with others, including those of other world faiths, who seek to address particular concerns from the needs of the inner city (Inner Cities Religious Council)[32] to the ethical implications of genetic research.

Raymond Fung's description of 'The Isaiah Agenda' (Isaiah 65, 20–23) is generally suggestive for social responsibility and applies to most faith communities. Fung writes: [33]

What is the Isaiah Agenda? It is concrete and clear in its objective. It specifies:
– that children do not die;
– that old people live in dignity;
– that those who build houses live in them;
– and those who plant vineyards eat the fruit.

[ISAIAH 65:20-23]

We want to communicate the following to our neighbours: 'The God we believe in is One who protects the children, empowers the elderly, and walks with working men and women. As Christians, we wish to act accordingly. We believe you share in similar concerns. Let us join hands.'

Practical spirituality will not be concerned with utopias or with an obsessional concern for the perfect ordering of society which is more the mark of some new religious movements. It will, nevertheless, work soundly and steadily for the achievement of justice and peace (Clarke).[34]

4

The Inter-relationship of
the Three Spiritualities

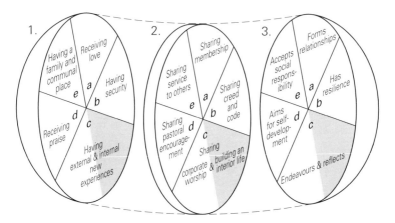

Figure 5 Spirituality: a dynamic, tripartite and inter-related concept

Many definitions of 'spirituality' are possible, but by their multiplicity these tend to create confusion rather than offer a clear structure for thinking.

The composite diagram above sets out spirituality as a tripartite and dynamically inter-related concept.

The tripartite and inter-related model attempts to illustrate two primary factors: (i) that while the three components, or types, of spirituality can theoretically be separated, they essentially belong together and interconnect, and (ii) that the five sub-components of each spirituality type have something of a common character running through them:

	'Being'	'Belonging'	'Behaving'
a	love	membership	relationships
b	security	shared norms	resilience
c	external and internal new experiences	corporate and private prayer	endeavour and reflection
d	praise	encouragement	development
e	communal place	service to others	social responsibility

> *Spirituality*, therefore, describes a healthy attitude towards and a positive pattern of engagement (i) with ourselves and our family; (ii) with our God and our faith community; and (iii) with our day-to-day activities and our involvement with others in the wider world.

A living and holistic spirituality needs a rhythm of receiving and giving, which a functioning devotional spirituality can assist in facilitating.

Clearly, every child or young person requires support for each type of his or her spirituality.

> *Spiritual needs* refer to a child or young person's human-spiritual needs of being valued and nurtured in a rounded way by their parents and family; to their devotional-spiritual needs of being integrated in a balanced manner within their own faith community, and of being affirmed in their distinctively personal expression of reverence; and to their practical-spiritual needs of being prepared for and having the opportunity to engage creatively, caringly and thoughtfully in everyday life.

It is important to understand the holistic reality that in all our attitudes and actions our human, devotional and practical spiritualities relate together, and that while congruence between them, and their components, should enhance health and happiness, dissonance between them will, in all probability, contribute to the opposite.

4.1 Interiority and values

Each spirituality component, or type, has within sub-component 'c' a section of 'interiority', i.e. of inner awareness, understanding or appreciation. In Figures 1, 2, 4 and 5 these are shown as shaded zones. (See also Appendix 1 where these sub-components are highlighted in italics.)

While spirituality is commonly referred to (e.g. in book shop and library classifications) as the interior zone of devotional spirituality, or perhaps less commonly to the interior zone of human spirituality, it is, as a whole, far broader than what these areas of 'interiority' represent.

Interiority, therefore, is not only the gradual development of a private and inner life of prayer and devotion but also, in human spirituality, a consciousness and inner appreciation and cherishing of goodness, joy, truth and beauty. In practical spirituality it embodies a readiness to reflect upon the principles and implications of one's actions – personal, interpersonal and corporate – and to be aligned and identified with certain key values.

A healthy human spirituality will provide a promising foundation for one's practical values, and an adequate devotional spirituality will serve to refresh and renew them.

4.2   *Relationships*

In practical spirituality our relationships will, in general, be of three kinds: (i) of intimacy with someone to whom we are committed; (ii) of friendship with those with whom we have things in common; and (iii) of association with those, for example, from the same school, club or choir, with whom we work alongside, identify with and are acquainted with to some extent, though not enough to have established a friendship. For children and some young people, relationships will consist mainly of friendship and association.

Three implications arise from this across all three components of spirituality. The first is that the richer and more well-rounded a person's experience of human spirituality has been, the better their prospects will be for forming balanced and undemanding friendships, and in due course for becoming committed to another in intimacy with sensitivity, loyalty and kindness.

The second is that the practice of devotional spirituality through faith community membership opens the door to two special categories of relationship: (i) one which falls between a family relationship and ordinary friendship (when a bond is formed with a member of the faith community which may be as close as that with a member of family), and (ii) one which is essentially a combination of friendship and association (since regular fellow worshippers, in many cases, will not quite be in the category of friends but are more familiar than mere acquaintences). These additional 'zones of relationship' will have potential benefits for a child or young person.

The third point is that a key aspect of an intimate relationship is the love, respect and concern shown by one party for the other.

The devotional-spiritual element preserves and protects these aspects. Its sub-components (see Figure 2) should allow a relationship of intimacy to have depth, space and sources of renewal and should promote respect for the other's individuality to safeguard against the destructive element of possessiveness. In addition, it should allow the unintrusive support of an informal network of people with a genuine interest in the welfare of any child which may be born.

Sex education in schools which places emphasis on the social skills of choice and the exercise of responsibility needs also to acknowledge the contribution which devotional spirituality has to make to those in a committed and intimate relationship.

Recent research by Mellaby et al. has shown that the level of teenagers' understanding of human sexuality limited their ability to make informed decisions.[35] An understanding of human sexuality should include an awareness about aspects of spirituality and how these may be seen to support the experience of intimacy within a committed relationship.

4.3   The primacy of human spirituality

A sound and healthy human spirituality is the essential foundation for a wholeness of spirituality overall. Helping a child to have a good start in life cannot be commended too highly.

The following excerpt from a British Council of Churches report speaks for itself in amplifying the sub-components of love and security in the life of a child, which are virtually irreplaceable: [36]

> ... the child who is brought up by normal, loving parents learns that whatever may be the standards by which he is judged in the great world outside, his family do not love him because they think him beautiful, or because he is intelligent or talented, or because he has a nice nature. They will take pleasure in any beauty or talent or attractiveness of disposition which he may possess, certainly, but they do not love him *because* of these things. They love him for no better reason than that he is theirs. The child knows, in a word, that his family's love for him is a love which he does not have to deserve, and which he can therefore count on. The experience of such a love, which shines on the just and the unjust, the responsible and the

irresponsible or prodigal, which does not have to be merited, is essential if we are ever to grasp, or be grasped by, the love of God in Christ. It is not itself, of course, *religious* experience, but it is the vital material out of which Christian understanding is formed.

The implicit principles here of 'acceptance', 'valuing' and 'identification' are highly significant.

4.4 *Outwardness and social responsibility*

Devotional spirituality has so far been taken to refer primarily to belonging to a local faith community. However, it would be a mistake to miss the important potential such membership may have in developing an attitude and frame of thinking which could help the individual child or young person come to terms with life in a complex and relatively heavily populated world, not least as far as the social responsibility component of practical spirituality is concerned.

As a member of a main faith community, a child or young person belongs to a group of people who, ideally, will have a commitment to fellowship with and the support of: (i) other members of their local faith community; (ii) members of other branches of their faith community in that country and overseas; (iii) members of other denominations of their faith community; (iv) members of other faith communities altogether – especially locally; (v) members of the local neighbourhood or community in general, including those not identified with any particular faith community; and (vi) others of national and international society in general.

These concerns will be shown variously through projects and activities shared with other faith communities, charity functions, friendships, meetings, teachings, and through attitudes in general, to provide but a few examples.

As a member of a local faith community, a child or young person will, ideally, have first-hand experience of membership of a group of people who have affinity with sections of their own faith community, but who also have a thoughtfully structured concern for the welfare of society as a whole.

While a child or young person without any affiliation to a main faith community may grow to have respect and concern for the welfare of others, practising membership of a healthy and caring faith community should give shape and enhancement to that attitude of goodwill in a particularly significant and effective way. Such assistance in coming to terms with living in fraternity with and respect for not only fifty or sixty million, but some five or six billion others, should not be dismissed lightly.

In contrast, a child or young person may sometimes be attracted to joining a gang, or other such group, through which they may discover something of a 'psuedo-religion' via the group's distinctive membership, sub-culture, ritual, support/revenge network and, possibly, selected altruistic cause. The group can offer a context of meaning, but this will very likely be short focused as well as being limited and temporary. Membership of a well-functioning main faith community should have the power to lift a young person to a vantage point where they will have a much longer-focused, broader, constructive and consistent outlook towards others.

More especially, it may show that those who do not profess any religion, but have a concern for community through their human spirituality, are 'walking in the shadows' of where devotional spirituality has concern and could give direction.

However, overall, if someone does not exemplify devotional spirituality, this does not mean that it is not an essential part of spirituality as a whole but that it is technically possible to live and experience human and practical spirituality without its particular potential and enrichment.

4.5 The process of 'becoming'

Grace Davie subtitles her recent book *Religion in Britain Since 1945* as 'believing without belonging'.[37] Devotional spirituality, as we have shown above, is certainly about belonging, and any trend away from that – towards the 'privatisation' of faith – is to be regretted.

But spirituality overall is about 'becoming' in the sense of being 'in process': open to growth, open to response, open to renewal and open to hope. This is applicable to every stage in life. Joe Hasler, interestingly, having applied the notion of 'belonging' to our community membership, interprets 'becoming' as the process of human development which involves both personal and corporate growth – human development being a process by which we are 'becoming human together'.[38] It may be argued that in participative membership of a sound and healthy faith community, such a process should be both facilitated and demonstrated.

Spiritual development overall means the ongoing and, to some extent, cyclical process by which (moving from left to right on Figure 5) our human spirituality (i) is established and grows in relationships with and concern for others; (ii) is extended into devotional spirituality, influenced by sound tradition and supported by membership of a faith community; and (iii) becomes integrated within a profile of practical spirituality – or day-to-day positive and interpersonal engagement in life – in a world for which we are both thankful, and also in which we are committed to contributing towards the struggle for the common good.

5

IMPLICATIONS FOR

SOCIAL WORK

It has been shown that for children, young people and adults, devotional spirituality – the expression of our selves, of our hopes and values, and our response to the Ultimate, in the culture and worship of our religion – is a follow-on and partner experience to our human spirituality, and, together with that, can become a formative factor in our practical spirituality, or lived-out attitudes and relationships in life.

The Children Act 1989 has mirrored this tripartite concept of spirituality to some extent. Section 1 refers to the 'welfare' of the child, by which we would assume the inclusion of his or her human-spiritual needs. Section 22(5)(c) includes consideration for 'the child's religious persuasion', by which we would mean devotional spirituality and section 24(1) stipulates that attention be paid to the young person's welfare on leaving care, by which we would include concern for his or her practical spirituality. (See Appendix 2.)

In the Children Act 1989 religious persuasion is usually referred to in conjunction with consideration of the child's racial origin, and cultural and linguistic background. These are all factors of identity, with religious persuasion being of particular significance.

It should be noted that the 1989 Act provides for religious persuasion to be taken into account in connection with a care order (section 33(6)(a)), voluntary homes (section 61(3)(c) and Schedule 5.7(2)(h)), and Registered Children's Homes (section 64(3)(c)). The Act also provides that religious persuasion shall be a consideration in the appointment of foster parents (Schedule 2.12(e)) and child minders (section 74(6)) for short or long-term arrangements.

Furthermore, in the sad event of a funeral, provision is made for religious custom, as regards burial or cremation, to be respected (Schedule 2.20(3)). In addition, the Act respects the provision of religious instruction under a trust deed in controlled or assisted community homes (section 55(5)).

However, concern for the consideration of the child's religious persuasion is greatly developed in *The Children Act 1989: Guidance and Regulations* and some seminal extracts are provided below which illustrate the careful and helpful thought which has been given to this. [39]

Volume 3, Family Placements and *Volume 4, Residential Care:*

Race, culture, religion and linguistic background

2.40. A child's ethnic origin, cultural background and religion are important factors for consideration. It may be taken as a guiding principle of good practice that, other things being equal and in the great majority of cases, placement with a family of similar ethnic origin and religion is most likely to meet a child's needs as fully as possible and to safeguard his or her welfare most effectively. Such a family is most likely to be able to provide a child with continuity in life and care and an environment which the child will find familiar and sympathetic and in which opportunities will naturally arise to share fully in the culture and way of life of the ethnic group to which he belongs. Where the aim of a placement is to reunite the child with his or her own family, contact and work with the family will in most cases be more comfortable for all and carry a greater chance of success if the foster parents are of similar ethnic origin. Families of similar ethnic origin are also usually best placed to prepare children for life as members of an ethnic minority group in a multi-racial society, where they may meet with racial prejudice and discrimination, and to help them with their development towards independent living and adult life.

2.41. These principles should be applied with proper consideration for the circumstances of the individual case. There may be circumstances in which placement with a family of different ethnic origin is the best choice for a particular child. In other cases such a placement may be the best available choice. For example, a child may have formed strong links with prospective foster parents or be related to them. Siblings or step siblings who are not all of the same ethnic origin may need placement together. A child may prefer and need to remain close to school, friends and family even though foster parents of the same ethnic origin cannot be found in the locality. A child with special needs may require carers with particular qualities or abilities, so that choice is limited.

The importance of religion as an element of culture should never be overlooked: to some children and families it may be the dominant factor, so that the religion of foster parents, for example, may in some cases be more important than their ethnic origin.

2.42. For a child whose parents are of different ethnic groups, placement in a family which reflects as nearly as possible the child's ethnic origins is likely to be the best choice in most cases. But choice will be influenced by the child's previous family experience and, as with all placement decisions, by the child's wishes and feelings. In discussing and exploring these with a child, responsible authorities should be ready to help the child with any confusion or mis-understandings about people of different ethnic groups which may have arisen through previous family or placement experience. Children of mixed ethnic origin should be helped to understand and take a pride in both or all elements in their cultural heritage and to feel comfortable about their origins. Carers must be able to provide this, with the help and sup-port of others where necessary. This applies equally whether a child is placed with a minority ethnic family or with a white family or a family including members of differing ethnic ori-gins. Where it has not proved possible to make a placement which entirely reflects the child's race and culture, an inde-pendent visitor could provide a link with the child's racial and cultural background (if the criteria for appointing an indepen-dent visitor apply).

Volume 3, Family Placements:

Assessment of potential foster parents

3.24. *Religion* and degree of religious observance and capac-ity to care for a child of a particular religion or from a more or less religious background than that of the foster parents: the social worker should seek to understand the extent to which religion influences the foster parent's family life. What is the element of familiarity and sympathy with and understanding of other denominations and faiths with which the foster family may have links through relatives and friends? What would be expected of a foster child by way of participation in the religious life of the family? Would this be compatible with the expectations and needs of a child and his parents? How would the applicant expect to participate in and nurture a child's religious life?

Volume 4, Residential Care:

Religious observance

1.121. Regulation 11 requires that each child is, as far as is practicable, to have an opportunity to attend such religious services and receive such instructions as are appropriate to the religious persuasion to which the child may belong. The regulation also requires that the child be provided with facilities for religious observance, for example special diets and clothing.

1.122. Persons in charge of children's homes should ensure that enquiries are made into the religious and cultural background of each child as part of planning the child's admission and settling in. Special efforts must be made to ensure that important aspects of a child's cultural and religious heritage are not lost at this crucial stage of his life. Enquiries should be made of the parents, those who looked after the child previously, persons in contact with the child and the local authority responsible for arranging accommodation. This information should be recorded in the child case record.

1.123. Positive steps should then be made to provide facilities to allow the child to practise his religion in a manner appropriate to his age. The extent to which care staff can do this directly will of course depend upon their own religious persuasion. It may be necessary to help a child make contact with a local church or group of adherents to the child's religion. Great sensitivity may be needed and the child's own family should be asked to assist. If the child is in close contact with his own family it is possible that he could join his family for religious services. A number of homes which are schools have been founded by particular religious groups. It is important that full details of the nature of religious observance are given in the schools' prospectus so that parents and children are fully aware of the religious background and practices of the school. It is also important that SSDs have such information so that they may be made aware of particular matters concerning religious observance and practice before visits are made.

1.124. It may be necessary to allow a child special privacy in order to pray during the course of the day, or to build a small shrine somewhere within the home. Obviously such requirements may impact on other children and will therefore need to be given careful consideration. The ideal may not be possible but it is essential that the need is recognised and the child feels that every possible consideration is being given to respect for his religion.

Catering arrangements

1.129. The menus provided should incorporate a reasonable choice, within the limits of the budget available to the home, to allow account to be taken of the individual preferences of children in the home. Each child in the home will have his own individual needs, which may relate to his racial, cultural or religious background, physical or other disability, or special dietary needs because of conditions such as diabetes. Account should therefore be taken of the particular needs of each child in the home, whatever they may be, and appropriate arrangements made.

Welfare

2.5. In undertaking that planning for a child in care the local authority is required to give the same attention to the wishes and feelings of the child, parents and others as they must when providing accommodation under voluntary arrangements. The local authority should also take into account and consider fully the child's religious persuasion, racial origin and cultural and linguistic background.

5.1 Respecting religious identity

Understandably, the Children Act 1989 does not itself spell out what making provision for, or giving consideration to, the religious persuasion of the child involves. However, the *Guidance and Regulations* does go towards clarifying this and refers to the nurture of the child in his or her religious persuasion.

Meeting the religious needs of a child or young person of an expressed religious persuasion may be summarised as follows:

1. helping them to be aware of their religious identity and to value what is considered best in their religious tradition;
2. providing opportunity for them to link up with others of their faith community and to share in worship together;
3. encouraging them to integrate, gradually and gently, their faith, their experiences, their attitudes, and their lifestyle.

This type of care requires certain skills in professional carers. Firstly, it calls for a disposition of *religious respect* and a willingness and generosity to become *attuned* to the essentials of a child or young person's own religious tradition.

Secondly, a sense of *discernment* is needed in order to be able to seek out a faith community of the religious persuasion in question which seems most appropriate for the child or young person. A *commitment* to devotional-spiritual well-being and development is also required, to the extent that the carer will encourage a young person's attendance by readiness for personal accompaniment, while having the *judgement* to know when to prompt a young person towards participation in worship according to their tradition and when not to.

Thirdly, it calls for *patience and openness* to the challenge of embodying an *example* of how faith, experience, attitude and lifestyle can be positively and happily integrated within a person's life (or at least being open and informative about someone who may be seen to do this in an exemplary way), and for *resourcefulness* in responding to questions or requests for advice in this regard.

It will be recognised that, for social workers or other carers, dismissive, thoughtless, negatively critical or cynically secularist attitudes must be regarded as totally unprofessional.

5.2 Pointers for religious care and support

Children or young people who are being looked after by a local authority or through a voluntary organisation should have an assessment of their devotional-spiritual needs as part of, and also to inform, their care plan:

1. The child or young person may require a programme of support, either to compensate for human-spiritual deprivation or to facilitate the healing of human-spiritual damage, or both. Support for devotional spirituality must take account of this.

2. The child or young person, although having a familial affinity with a faith community, in practice may have had no meaningful contact with it and therefore supporting a child's religious upbringing would, in such a case, mean re-commencing or even commencing it. Attention should be given to providing a simple programme offering the child a variety of suitable opportunities for affiliation as part of their care plan. The particular and existing religion of a young person in care must be respected (Wyld).[40]

3. The child or young person may, in an extreme case, have been rejected by their faith community, either themselves or on account of their families. The assumption, therefore, of ongoing association may be problematic, and an alternative local faith community may have to be found.[41]

4. A child or young person who has been exposed to a highly secularised and perhaps deviant sub-culture, and who may also have severe personal difficulties, would not be easy for a local faith community to integrate. A care worker might be in a position to offer some guidance to the faith community without breach of confidentiality.

5. In giving consideration to 'the child's religious persuasion, racial origin and cultural and linguistic background' it is the concern of the local authority that the child has associations with a sound and typical example of his or her religion, racial group, culture and language. One of the objects of this is to help the child or young person to have pride in these elements of his or her heritage.

6. The child or young person should have their/their parents' religious persuasion clearly recorded with any indication of degree of membership or practising status.

7. Confidentiality and privacy should be observed when introducing a child or young person to a faith community, but an authorised befriender or the key worker could be indicated to the faith community leadership.

8. An unconsidered choice against religion should be treated with patience, sensitivity and judicious judgment to keep the matter under review, since, with regard to his or her age and understanding, the child may not appreciate the potential network of

solidarity, values and support he or she may be jettisoning. The child in this case should be assisted to regard themselves as a temporarily non-practising adherent and the matter kept suitably under review.

9. A child or young person who has experienced severe trauma may possibly have arrived at an image of God as 'Absence, Abuse or Unfeeling Judge' (with the companion emotions of fear, anger and rejection). Such a child will need skilled support and understanding so that he or she is able to move on from such aberration and have sound and truthful faith community experiences, so that he or she is equipped to surmount subsequent difficulties and gain the ability to cope with life (practical spirituality).[42]

5.3 Some cautions in religious care

While the care plan for any child or young person should be informed by an assessment of their devotional-spiritual needs, this should be modified by certain principles for the protection of the particular child's religious welfare:

1. Religious observance should not be promoted for a child or young person in isolation so that they stand out as the only religiously practising person.

2. Religious observance should not be required to be privatised so that a child or young person is constrained to retire to 'a private place,' unless he or she so desires.

3. Provision for religious observance, religious instruction, dietary and dress facilities etc., should not simply be regarded as the right of those of minority faiths.

4. Religious observance and instruction may well raise issues (e.g. about gender) which may conflict with and test more commonly accepted viewpoints. The care situation should always promote good practice and not treat any young person as inferior to another.

5. Provision for a plurality of religious observance, instruction, dietary and dress facilities, etc., requires an expressed and suitably publicised statement of hospitality to those of all faiths.

The information in the booklet *Concise Guide to the Customs of Ethnic Minority Religions in Hampshire* dealing with beliefs, diet, dress, language, social rules, naming systems, birth and death customs, is particularly helpful in this regard.[43]

6. Religious observance in the case of the child whose parents are of different religions will require special sensitivity. It may be that the family and child have opted for a bi-religious approach, but while this would be likely to place the child at a disadvantage from becoming a full member of either faith, observance must be at the discretion of the child.

7. It should not be assumed that a voluntary agency of an expressed faith tradition would be unacceptable to those of other faith traditions. To quote from the briefing *Children Act 1989: Day Care of Children Under 8 Years of Age* produced by PCCA – Promoting Christian Child Care Alternatives: [44]

What local authorities often do not understand is that parents from other faiths sometimes prefer their children to be brought up in a Christian environment (where there is a belief in God and a set of values) than in the local authority equivalent. Also, that parents are unlikely to be expecting you to teach their religious faith.

8. At a time of stress, trauma and disruption it could be understandable for some children to want to withdraw and dissociate themselves from others and from settings which may have painful associations. Some may even be tempted towards sacrilegious expression. A cry for space should not be confused with a full intellectual declaration of dissent.

9. Counselling must always observe the principle of ethical respect, well-expressed by Felix Biestek: [45]

The caseworker, especially when he is of a different religion than the client, must respect the conscience of the client and help the client make choices and decisions which are within the boundaries of that conscience. If the client violates the moral law and acts contrary to his conscience, he does spiritual harm to himself. This not only produces psychological difficulties for the client, such as guilt feelings, but it also does spiritual damage. The caseworker needs to have a real conviction about the ontological reality of spiritual values. The caseworker is not promoting the total welfare of the client if he helps the client to solve a social or emotional problem by means which are contrary to the client's philosophy of life.

5.4 Religious care and those with disabilities

It is important to note that young people with disabilities and those with learning difficulties should be encouraged to share equally with others in the benefits of membership of a faith community. They can share on a basis similar to everyone else in membership, tradition, worship, service and community. The work of SPRED, the Special Education Division of the Archdiocese of Chicago, has been outstanding in providing an 'inclusive' approach to those with learning difficulties.[46]

However, these young people may require special provision in the support of their devotional spirituality.

Firstly, they will need to be treated as normal members of their faith community, without having attention unduly focused upon them on the one hand or being left in the background on the other. They should be welcomed as equal members of the religious fellowship, and indeed as being recognised for their own distinctive gift(s).

The UN Convention on the Rights of the Child 1989, Article 23.3, provides for the needs of those with disabilities for spiritual development:

> ...and shall be designed to ensure that the disabled child has effective access to and receives education, training, health care services, rehabilitation services, preparation for employment and recreation opportunities in a manner conducive to the child's achieving the fullest possible social integration and individual development, including his or her cultural and spiritual development.

This needs to be opened up in individual cases in order to consider such a young person's human-spiritual, devotional-spiritual and practical-spiritual needs.

The hallmark of a faith community with members or visitors with disabilities or learning difficulties is that they extend to them a welcome, access, appropriate explanation of any act of worship and a place of belonging. Papers in relation to religion made available at the time of the International Year of Disabled People are still valuable for insights and advice.[47, 48, 49]

5.5 Practising tolerance and respect

> The attitude of a local authority or voluntary agency towards the provision of religious care should be to hold in balance a *quadrilateral of obligations:* (i) to the religious persuasion of the child; (ii) to the wishes of the child; (iii) to the expectations of parents and faith community; and (iv) to the principle contained in the UN Convention on the Rights of the Child 1989, about an attitude of tolerance and respect for those of other faiths.

A voluntary agency whose foundation is related to a specific religion may legitimately create an ethos of that faith and its values in its homes, schools or projects, provided that at the same time it accepts the quadrilateral of obligations in religious care set out above. The key point is that its values and approach should be clarified in a mission or other purpose statement which is properly available.

The following quotation from Manazir Ahsan may be seen to speak for all faith communities: [50]

> It is to be noted that the new Children Act, promulgated in October 1991, is an important breakthrough, as – among other things – it includes, for the first time, considerations of race, religion, ethnic and linguistic background and makes it unlawful to neglect these factors when arranging for any child to be cared for. Local authorities and child care agencies are, therefore, urged to take all necessary measures to safeguard and foster the religious aspirations of children in care, and not to attempt to subvert or undermine the child's faith, culture and language. This study powerfully advocates the needs of Muslim children and young persons in care to preserve their distinct identity as Muslims.

However, the consideration of racial origin, religious persuasion, culture and linguistic background cannot obviate the need for intercultural and inter-religious recognition, friendship and solidarity, as expressed, for example, in the Commonwealth Day Observance at Westminster Abbey each Spring. The care situation must provide 'hospitality' to those of all faiths and outlooks, and requires a spirit of generosity and understanding. Attention given to the food menus and requirements of those of different world faiths (Paraiso et al.), and to such matters as customs in caring for the dying (Neuberger), will have great significance in interfaith goodwill and understanding.[51, 52]

It is to be welcomed that the Department of Health's *Looking After Children* materials, launched in May 1995, include questions about religion in the assessment and action record under the category of 'identity'.[53] However, three points should be made in this connection:

1. The religious persuasion of the child is so much part of his or her social identity that space for such faith affiliation should be shown on the front of the record itself.

2. Appropriate questions about the recognition of support for the faith affiliation of the child ought to be included in the assessment and action records of Age Under One Year, Age One and Two Years, and Age Three and Four Years, and not only (and simply in respect of carers) commence at Age Five to Nine Years.

3. The questions to the child or young person in the Age Ten to Fourteen Years Assessment and Action Record, and in that for the Age Fifteen Years and Over, whilst commendably broader, could merit from the question 'Do you have enough opportunities to attend religious services?' being supplemented by a further question on opportunities for involvement in other faith community activities, such as a youth club, interest group or uniformed organisation.

In *Looking After Children: Research into Practice*, Harriet Ward comments in a manner which underscores the functional value of faith community membership, or of faith community activity involvement: [54]

> Although most looked after children were said to have some close friends, the majority of these friends were also in care or accommodation. Although immensely strong and supportive relationships can be formed in the face of shared adversity, vulnerable children and young people also need opportunities to interact with peers from a range of circumstances. Children whose main source of friendship is with others who share the low expectations, poor self-esteem and low achievements that

characterise so many of those who are looked after tend to become marginalised and alienated from mainstream society and derive their social identity, values and mores from an increasingly narrow group.

A study on policies on ethical, linguistic and religious needs in Wales highlights the principle of taking into consideration feedback from people themselves rather than simply assuming that we know what is best for them.[55] In itself, this is a mark of consideration and respect and can be easily overlooked in the case of children and young people:

> The kind of data needed for sensitive planning cannot be obtained by merely counting heads. What is required is a needs assessment *from the perspective of the service user*, including not only quantitative but also qualitative data.

Meeting the religious needs of the child and young person in the field of social work requires considerable sensitivity and empathy, though it should be seen as a quite normal and natural part of the concept of care. It is appreciated that accredited general background information will be a valuable professional resource. In this regard, the work currently in progress for the publication in 1996 of a training pack on the religious and spiritual needs of children and their families in receipt of personal social services, on behalf of the Central Council for Education and Training in Social Work (CCETSW), is to be greatly welcomed.

A list of useful references to religious care in *The Children Act 1989: Guidance and Regulations* can be found in Appendix 3.

6

IMPLICATIONS FOR

EDUCATION

Education is a vital setting for the development of the potential of the child, and for the drawing out of his or her capacities and the enlargement of his or her horizons. The partnership between home and school, or care setting and school, is an essential one – strikingly illustrated in a residential special school where the co-operation of parents, care staff and teachers is so essential. However, this is only part of the wider trio of child support provided by home, school and faith community.

The comment in the Dearing Report that 'by showing strong interest in their child's achievement, by encouraging reading, by taking advantage of every day occurrences to widen the child's understanding and knowledge, all parents can help greatly' reinforces the role of school and parent together in supporting aspects of a child's human spirituality, not least sub-components 'c' and 'd' – new experience and praise.[56]

6.1 Promoting human spirituality

It is noted with approval that in the Education Reform Act 1988 'spiritual' precedes the other adjectives applied to 'development' (section 1(2)(a)). (See Appendix 4.)

However, when the National Curriculum Council Discussion Paper *Spiritual and Moral Development* sets out an assorted list of spiritual factors, on analysis it fails to differentiate between 'human', 'devotional' and 'practical' spirituality and therefore is of restricted usefulness: [57]

	(See figure 5:)
beliefs	(2 (b))
a sense of awe, wonder and mystery	(1 (c) interiority)
experiencing feelings of transcendence	(1 (c) interiority)
search for meaning and purpose	(1 (b) and (e))

self knowledge	(3 (d))
relationships	(3 (a))
creativity	(3 (c))
feelings and emotions	(1 (a) and (d))

'Beliefs' can be taken to mean merely 'understandings about the world and society', but more properly these refer to the way in which human-spiritual experience and convictions can be taken forward, correlated and appropriated through the vehicle of a religious creed, hence the cross-referencing above. The weight of the components listed above can be seen to lie in the field of human spirituality with devotional spirituality virtually by-passed.

The school has a significant part to play in promoting all components of human spirituality by the way it values pupils in its mission statement, and by the way this is applied and implemented across the life of the school, for example in pastoral care. The school also has a function to support a pupil's devotional and practical spirituality. This is a much broader approach and undertaking than that of the Ofsted (Office for Standards in Education) Framework for Inspection (revised August 1993 edition) which concentrated on the interiority of one aspect of spirituality, namely human spirituality: [58]

> Spiritual development relates to that aspect of inner life through which pupils acquire insights into their personal existence which are of enduring worth. It is characterised by reflection, the attribution of meaning to experience, valuing a non-material dimension to life and intimations of an enduring reality. 'Spiritual' is not synonymous with 'religious'; all areas of the curriculum may contribute to pupils' spiritual development.

This extract reinforces the beginning of an unfortunate tendency, which will have the effect of reducing the experience of devotional spirituality in schools in favour of the 'interiority' sub-component of human spirituality. It is important in itself, but not at the expense of other aspects of spirituality.

However, promoting spirituality in all its three forms is no bland exercise. As a seminar sponsored by the Cambridge Islamic Academy in response to the NCC discussion paper pointed out: [59]

> Nevertheless there is a dark side to our corporate life which cannot safely be disregarded. Embedded in it are tragic elements which are highly destructive of human sensibilities

and which can brutalise humans' treatment of each other, foster aggression and injustice and, through greed and short-sightedness, help to destroy the living world which we inhabit and of which we are part. Nor are educational establishments immune from such malign influences. For, as any experienced teacher knows, schools too have their share of bullying, selfishness, intolerance, discrimination and the like.

Any characterisation of spiritual development has, therefore, to recognise that it also involves the development of a strong set of values which can help counter these negative forces in human experience and encourage a readiness to oppose them. Without such over-riding values the quest for spirituality can all too easily degenerate into an unwarranted kind of aesthetic or emotional escapism from the harsher realities of life.

6.2 Supporting devotional spirituality

Collective worship (see Education Reform Act 1988, section 6 in Appendix 4) should logically be devised so as to support and assist in the expression of the devotional spirituality of members of the educative community.

As the Department of Education Circular 94/81, *Religious Education and Collective Worship* states, '"worship" is not defined in the legislation and in the absence of any such definition it should be taken to have its natural and ordinary meaning' (paragraph 57).[60]

In contrast, it is interesting that John M Hull in *School Worship: An Obituary* appeared to argue for the county school assembly being directed towards the building up of what this book would call human spirituality – rather than giving expression to devotional spirituality (see chapter 6 and especially pages 132–134).[61] However, such an approach would blend well with the supporting of a child suffering either human–spiritual deprivation or damage.

The following quotation from the Chairman of the Board of Education of the General Synod of the Church of England suggests a slightly different emphasis, giving room to some interiorisation in human spirituality, but encroaching upon exploration of practical spirituality:[62]

Speaking in a personal capacity, the Rt Rev David Young, the Bishop of Ripon, last week told *The TES* that collective worship could have meaning for many more pupils and teachers if schools ceased to concentrate solely on traditional forms of words, focusing instead on spiritual development in assemblies. 'I would want to make strong links between the emphasis in the '88 Act on spiritual growth, and the place of collective worship' he said last week. 'By the word spiritual I'm meaning something like the development of the interior person, the development of creativity and motivation, as well as the academic or learning skills. I would be looking for opportunities to explore experiences of community, experiences of success and failure, of grief – all these important experiences which are part of living. They are also educational experiences. There is a great deal to explore: ideas of the transcendental, of symbol, or of form silence, reflection, as well as words.'

However, one would expect collective worship to primarily express devotional spirituality.

The paper 'Worship Assembly in the Multi-Faith School: A Proposal for a New Approach' by John Bradford, in *Discernment*, took forward the appropriateness 'for a learning community to make special provision for the expression of the religious beliefs and values of its members' (see page 17).[63] The paper recommended, as a new and fundamental principle 'that the religious tradition observed in school worship assembly should be in proportion to the number of pupils of any world faith in the school, with those of other world faiths being present in respectful attendance.'

In the light of this it would be appropriate for special training to be provided for teachers in giving assemblies which might promote an understanding of devotional spirituality.

Section 9(1) of the Education Reform Act 1988 (see Appendix 4) provides that, 'It shall not be required as a condition of any pupil attending any maintained school, that he shall attend or abstain from attending any Sunday School or any place of religious worship.' One implication of this provision is that what happens in Religious Education in school should be complementary to what happens in any faith community instruction class, rather than antithetical to it.

While for some it is important to press for proper observance of school worship according to law, for others it is more important that the logistical and timetable difficulties which arise are addressed, for example in a large comprehensive school. However, a crucial issue which is all too often completely overlooked is the value of collective worship for the pupil who is experiencing real difficulties at home, or who is in care. Four benefits may be identified:

1. For pupils who are in care, either in a foster or residential home, school worship can be a treasured moment of looking beyond their own immediate circumstances, and of being uplifted by a sense of the Divine and by the challenge of the adventure of life as a whole.

2. For the pupil whose life has been significantly disturbed or disrupted by the illness of a parent or by bereavement, by the divorce or separation of parents or by the long-term absence of (or even lack of knowledge of) a parent, school worship can offer a serious and neutral place where, privately, a prayer can be said for those secretly most dear.

3. For the pupil who suffers pressure, unpredictability and disruption at home, school worship can be an oasis of peace, an experience of fraternity and an expression of 'order'. God can be met as the One who brings both outer harmony and inner stillness.

4. For the pupil who has suffered victimisation or abuse and who has a very low sense of self-worth, or who has low self-esteem for some other reason, school worship can be a time of reassurance and encouragement through the collective celebration of God's love and concern for each individual – not just for the 'top-scorers,' the 'best-lookers' or the group-leaders.

Of course, in a multifaith society, school worship must be led in ways that take account of the proportions of the different main world religions represented in the school. When the language of another religion is being used, those of other faiths can be helped to silently re-interpret this in the context of their own.

These practical challenges should never be allowed to distract us from the deep intrinsic value of quality school worship for children and young people with family or personal difficulties of any kind.

School staffs who resist personally *leading* worship assembly, which they are entitled to do on the grounds of their own conscientious position, nevertheless have a residual duty to *manage the organisation* of collective worship for pupils which is appropriate and sincere.

6.3 Encouraging practical spirituality

Religious Education which encourages the study of 'models' – i.e. persons who have combined their human spirituality and their devotional spirituality, and have lived out their lives with a distinguished practical spirituality – may be said to serve a particularly useful function.

Religious Education which is purely analytic, examining forms of knowledge and categories of belief in a purely descriptive manner, may be educationally valid but is deficient for meeting the spiritual needs and encouraging the spiritual potential of the child or young person.

In his address to the RE Council in May 1992, David Pascall, Chairman of NCC, defined the spiritual as follows: [64]

> Let me be clear that I do not interpret this as applying only to the development of religious beliefs, or to any sort of conversion to a faith. To limit spirituality in this way would be to exclude from its scope the majority of pupils in our school who do not come from overtly religious homes. Such a definition would also alienate many teachers who do not profess a faith. Rather, I take the term as applying to something fundamental in the human condition which is not necessarily expressed through everyday language. It has to do with relationships with other people and, for believers, with God. It has to do with the universal search for individual identity – with our response to challenging experiences of life, such as death, suffering, beauty and the rare encountering of real goodness – it is to do with the search for meaning in life and values by which to live.

Pascall is unusual in that he appears to be centring upon aspects of practical spirituality as well as the interior component of human spirituality, but he seeks to leapfrog over devotional spirituality altogether, which, in Religious Education, is extremely curious.

The following quotation by Michael Walker, from the Christian tradition, is a useful example of practical spirituality: [65]

> The recognition that body, mind and soul must walk in step is one of the gifts that has been made to us by the great teachers of Christian prayer. The desert fathers, those pragmatic forefathers of the monastic movement, embarked upon a life designed to simplify the Christian response to the gospel and

thereby to simplify themselves. Dedicated to a life of prayer they yet stressed that prayer was to be rooted in the practical. A brother who swept the cell and prepared the meals did a no less worthy work for God than one who praised God in his pain and another who spent his days in contemplative prayer. Thomas Merton reminds us that the most awesome of all the Christian mystics, St John of the Cross, taught that the life of prayer was to be rooted in the daily acceptance of our ordinary duties in life. As soon as we begin to decontextualise spiritual experiences, whether they be prayer, worship or meditation, then we reverse the true direction of the Christian life and pass God on the way, for in Christ he plunged himself into the depths and recesses of the human experience and there revealed his glory.

6.4 Furthering faith development

The Education Reform Act 1988, sections 7(5)(a) and (b) (see Appendix 4) rightly makes provision for the consideration of a child's circumstances, age and aptitude in relation to collective worship. This has relevance to children in care who are attending school.

Although influential among certain specialists in Religious Education in the UK, theories of faith development seem to have more to do with ideological and moral development than with spiritual development, though the former can illuminate the cyclical process of movement through human spirituality, devotional spirituality and practical spirituality.

The work of James W Fowler of Emory University, Atlanta, Georgia, USA, has the following scheme as the core of faith development: [66]

Stage 0:	'Nursed Faith' or 'Foundation Faith' (The stuggle to trust and resist mistrust)	Age 0–4
Stage 1:	'Chaotic Faith' or 'Unordered Faith' (Imitating dependable adults in episodic ways)	Age 4–8
Stage 2:	'Ordering Faith' (Learning the stories of one's group and community)	Age 7–11

Stage 3:	'Conforming Faith' (Identifying with the views and opinions of others)	Age 12–18
Stage 4:	'Choosing Faith' (Critically reflecting on what and how one believes)	Age 18–40
Stage 5:	'Balanced Faith' or 'Inclusive Faith' (Living with paradoxes and polarities)	Age 30+
Stage 6:	'Selfless Faith' (Envisioning a sense of the unity of all things)	Later life

It should be noted that progression from stage to stage is not simply automatic; not many reach the higher stages and the attainment of Stage 6 is very rare.

Fowler is thought to lay too much emphasis on the cognitive aspect in the early stages, and is open to criticism for taking a somewhat 'de-religioned' interpretation of 'faith' and to reinforcing a generally 'individualised' position.

However, finding – or being found by – God should not merely be thought of as the goal of a lifelong pilgrimage or the culmination of passing through a series of stages of development. Indeed, a Wordsworthian approach to such a view might be that the chances become increasingly elusive as childhood passes. [67]

> But trailing clouds of glory do we come
> From God, who is our home:
> Heaven lies about us in our infancy!
> Shades of the prison-house begin to close
> Upon the growing Boy

David Heller writes in a similar vein: [68]

> Through their God representation, the children teach us much about the world and about our beliefs concerning the world. They tell us that the world has a personality all its own, filled with joy and pleasure. They demonstrate to us that the world is vastly complex; it presents constant socialization and at the same time it calls for great spontaneity. The children intimate to us that the world is filled with contradictions, not the least of which is faith and doubt in a deity. And the children seem to say, 'If in reality there is a deity,' and they seem to whisper that there is, 'then it may well turn out to be the Children's God.'

A key function of a school will be to assist in the drawing out of a pupil's faith potential and to value their insights and religious experiences rather than underplaying them. A pupil's right to privacy in this area should be honoured.

The impact of the full range of human-spiritual, devotional-spiritual and practical-spiritual needs apply at every stage of development and all three aspects of spirituality have interpersonal and community features as well as individual ones.

Of all faith development theories, the four-stage schema set out by John H Westerhoff III (see section 2.3, page 21 of this book) is probably the most straightforward and most closely correlated with devotional spirituality. Faith development in its narrower sense really requires a child or young person to have some fluency in the language and story of their own religion as a foundation on which to build.

6.5 Upholding tolerance and respect

The UN Convention on the Rights of the Child 1989, affirms the need for tolerance and respect for those of minority groups.

More especially, perhaps, children and young people need suitable opportunities to understand, in an informed and authentic way, what adherence to another main world religion (or to another main denomination) means for a child or young person of that persuasion 'from the inside'.

However, respect for the faith position of parents, children and young people of the majority, in a country which has an established religion, is not to be neglected either (see Education Reform Act 1988, section 8(3) in Appendix 4).

While consideration must be given to the wishes of parents who specifically request that their child be excluded from collective worship or religious education (see Education Reform Act 1988, section 9 in Appendix 4), the irony here is (i) that religious education is, in the main, far from 'indoctrinatory'; (ii) that for the older child the freedom to exercise his or her choice and judgement may thus be infringed; (iii) that the value of religion for their subsequent well-being may be denied; and (iv) that an experience of a spirit of tolerance and respect may be missed.

Schools should understand that a pupil's growth in devotional spirituality is an aspect of personal identity and of parental and faith community nurture, which it is the corporate responsibility of the school to foster and respect. Two provisos should be taken into account: (i) that allowance be made for the age, stage of development and social/domestic circumstances of the child, and (ii) that such fostering and respect should not be prejudicial to the fostering and respect due to any other pupil having a different faith identity.

As Rabbi Jonathan Sacks has said in his Reith Lectures: [69]

> Religions are the structures of our common life. In their symbols and ceremonies, the lonely self finds communion with others who share a past and future and a commitment to both. In their visions, we discover the worth of un-self-interested action, and find, in the haunting words of the Rabbi of Kotzk, that God exists wherever we let Him in. Education and inspiration will renew our communities of faith. The question will be whether they can be revived without the intolerances that once made religion a source of prejudice as well as pride.

It is of note that Crown Prince Hassan of Jordan, who became the first non-Christian to preach at Christ Church Cathedral, Oxford, on 4 June 1995, called for tolerance between Islam, Christianity and Judaism, which, he said, share common roots and aims.

It is a feature of particular sadness where countries which have once enjoyed religious heterogeneity and mutual respect (e.g. in the Sudan) fail to maintain and support religious freedom and tolerance.[70] Separatism or aggressive fundamentalism is the antithesis of tolerance. Peter Mitchell says, 'We ought, therefore, to add to the aims of education, or the work of such institutions as schools, the further task of facilitating this dialogue'.[71]

7

IMPLICATIONS FOR

FAITH COMMUNITIES

In the care of children and young people, and in the development of their human, devotional and practical spirituality, three institutions have a vital part to play: the home, the school and the faith community.

In contrast to some voluntary sector homes of a Christian or religious foundation, and also to public institutions such as hospitals or prisons, there has been no system of formal chaplaincy to local authority children's homes. Furthermore, these days the notion of chaplaincy, with its association with 'institutions', is not seen as helpful in connection with children's homes, which should have been, as far as possible, de-institutionalised.

A demerit of this situation is that, in many cases, faith communities have not been drawn close to children's homes and residential projects and it may often therefore be difficult for a young person to express a wish to reach out to their local faith community and to have contact with it.

In the past a child or young person from a care situation was seen, not infrequently, by the faith community to have carried some sort of stigma. Certainly, a generation ago, children from voluntary sector homes would have attended their faith community in uniform, sat together and been identified as a separate entity.

A faith community today has to move completely beyond these past practices. Members need to be alert to their responsibility to reach out to and welcome any child or young person in care locally who is of the same faith community and who wishes to receive its friendship and support. Where home has been problematic, and further problems may have been encountered at school, the 'extended family' of the faith community may have a special part to play in providing an environment which is free of complications or disruption of any sort.

It should be remembered that a faith community can only support a young member in having a positive relationship with those of other faith communities if it sets an example in interfaith community co-operation or dialogue.[72] The leaflet *Building Good Relations with People of Different Faiths* is useful for home, church, school, community centre, community project or other setting.[73]

7.1 *Having positive attitudes towards young people*

It is very easy for a local faith community, which has to be seriously attentive to such matters as the provision and maintenance of buildings, the celebration and leadership of worship, personal ministry to its adult members, and the raising of sufficient income, to overlook the needs of children and young people in general – especially those who have exceptional difficulties and who may make exceptional demands.

Faith communities who wish to respond to children and young people of their religious persuasion in local care settings must, above all else, have a positive attitude to the children and young people in the local neighbourhood. Children and young people must not be seen by a faith community as intrinsically difficult, lazy, a nuisance or a distraction to be controlled.

Children and young people in general must be seen by a local faith community as their prime resource, as a special gift, as equal members who have great potential for creativity, energy, helpfulness and loyalty. They should be seen as the valued foundation for the future as, for example, Cardinal Edouard Gagnon has expressed in a paper 'The Child is Also the Future of the Church'.[74]

Positive attitudes to children should be encouraged and reinforced among all the main world faiths, and a valuable resource for informing our understanding in this task is the section 'The Child in Different Religious Cultures' (Christian, Jewish, Islamic, Buddhist, and Indian) contained in the *Proceedings of the Eighth International Conference Organized by the Pontifical Council for Pastoral Assistance to Health Care Workers* (Vatican City, 1993).[75]

Only a faith community which makes this attitude shift in favour of children and young people can be in a safe and strong position to welcome those with special needs.

The report *Unfinished Business: Children and the Churches* indicates that churchgoers undervalue what children bring to the life of a Christian community. It expresses the point that true childhood, as an age of innocence and play, may only last a few years; exposure through the media to warfare, violence, human deprivation, sex and consumerism means that halfway through primary school young people become 'adult-children'.[76] If the report is correct then the case for the necessity of constructing positive attitudes towards children and young people may be a strong one. Doubtless, this viewpoint would have applicability to all faith communities.

7.2 Offering programmes for young people

A faith community should, of course, integrate children and young people in all its activities and acts of worship and value them as fellow members of the faith community. As soon as appropriate, young people should be included in the committee or management group which deals with the local faith community's affairs. However, it is appropriate that a faith community develops special programmes for children and young people which enhance their participation and involvement, and the satisfaction and enjoyment from this which may be obtained.

A programme for young people should meet the three aspects of their spirituality:

1. There should be activities which support their human spirituality, i.e. which give opportunity for meeting others, for friendship, play and recreation.
2. There should be activities which support their devotional spirituality, i.e. which provide opportunity for being deepened in faith and devotion.
3. There should be activities which support their practical spirituality, i.e. which not only provide opportunity for consideration and discussion about the wider issues of everyday life, but which also involve practical activities of service in the community – where possible in conjunction with young people of other faith communities.

These programmes should have a sufficient degree of openness to allow young people of the faith community, or those associated with the faith community and from different backgrounds and circumstances, to take part and to feel at home.

A key task for all faith communities is to develop 'a preferential option for young people'.[77] Harriet Ward indicates how children living with their families profit from a wide range of services provided by both public institutions and voluntary organisations, although there is considerable regional variation in their quality. She instances a wide range of leisure activities offered by both the local authority and the local church, and observes that where there is less provision, children 'tended to make less varied use of their leisure time and to watch more television'.[78]

Exeter Diocese Children and Young People's Committee 'Vision Statement' incorporates very well the principle of participation: [79]

All people are equal before God and so children and young people are respected and rooted in the Christian Community.

As with all ages in the Church, children and young people enjoy taking a full part in the regular worship of the community.

Children and young people are valued for their contribution to the decision making process in their local church regarding worship, evangelism, organisation, finance and the full life of the Church community.

Children and young people, young adults, the middle-aged, senior citizens, the disadvantaged, all sorts and conditions of people belong, are valued, and are contributing for the good of the whole Church.

Children and young people as members of the Christian community contribute to its honesty, relevance and responsiveness to the continuing needs of the community at large.

7.3 Understanding spiritual poverty

It is important for a faith community to understand the state of mind and heart of the child or young person who has had a disturbed or distressing background. Faith communities can be good at understanding those in later life who have met with difficulty or distress, but are not always so good with children, who may not immediately appear distressed and with whom conversation and contact may not be as usual.

Faith communities should not be encouraged to pry into or be unduly inquisitive about a child or young person's background or affairs. However, three basic marks of spiritual poverty should be recognised and understood:

1. If a child or young person has been abused, demeaned, neglected and made to feel worthless, he or she may find it very difficult to trust – let alone love – another person, especially another adult. They may have a tendency towards isolationism. They will need understanding and support in their human spirituality.
2. If a child or young person has had no contact with religious faith, if religion has always been ridiculed at home, or worse, if the young person has prayed for some abuse to stop and the abuse has continued, then the meaning and truth of worship may be very difficult for them to come to terms with at all. They will need understanding and support in their devotional spirituality.
3. If a child or young person has had a highly dislocated and problematic background, then he or she may find it very difficult to build up a coherent and cohesive interpretation of life. There may be a tendency towards dislocation and fragmentation in thinking and a degree of the erratic in behaviour and relationships. They will need understanding and support in their practical spirituality.

7.4 Showing flexibility and understanding

Bearing the content of the previous section in mind, it should be underscored that a child or young person from a difficult background needs some latitude and flexibility on the part of the faith community, rather than rigidity and accentuated direction.

One example may be the case of a Christian chorister, a very keen and young member of his church choir, who has to attend choir practices, church services, weddings and other special services, and courses which take place at Cathedrals and festivals. Punctuality, regularity and dependability are essential. His parents are divorced and he spends one weekend with his father and one with his mother. His mother strongly supports his choir attendance but his father forgets or overlooks it because it does not fit in with the activities of his new family. Either the Director of Music of the faith community in question must make allowances and be understanding about an, in effect, half-time chorister, which breaks all the rules (and which many of his fellow choristers may resent or wish to copy), or he must say that the arrangement is just not workable and deeply disappoint the boy. Hopefully, if the local faith community is attuned to being understanding and flexible in such cases, the partial attendance will be allowed to continue – with encouragement for attendance to be maximised so far as possible, especially as the boy grows older and can exercise more choice for himself.

Another example may be the case of a young person from a children's home who, because of past care placements and experiences, has an affinity with one denomination because that was the denomination of a carer of whom he was especially fond. However, this is forbidden by his natural mother. He is also undergoing personal one-to-one instruction by a minister of another denomination and is a bell-ringer at the church of yet another denomination. These anomalies have to be understood and given time to resolve themselves naturally, the pro-devotional spirituality disposition being seen overall as a positive.

The Children Act 1989 does make allowance for a community leader to be involved in the planning for a child's placement and to be consulted in the child's review (see under 'consultation' in the list of references to *The Children Act 1989: Guidance and Regulations,* Appendix 1). However, a child or young person must surely have the right to request his or her minister of religion, or other church leader, to act in this capacity. If so, the minister or other leader would hopefully have the generosity to be prepared to assist in promoting the welfare of the child or young person whose 'religious profile' was not quite as tidy as they might have preferred.

The following are five actions which faith communities can undertake to foster resilience in children and their families:

1. Faith communities should affirm the value of established and humane religious tradition as a vital cultural reserve to be depended on at all times, especially during periods of hardship.
2. Local congregations of faith communities should be open to those subject to difficult circumstances and display an attitude of supportiveness and constructive understanding.
3. Local congregations should strive to earn the respect of the young by their genuineness, their sincerity, their tradition, and by the simple beauty and regular observance of their worship.
4. Priests and ministers of religion should be aware of their role and potential for influencing those who are facing hardship.
5. Faith communities should work for the advocacy of child-centredness. There is a particular responsibility of those working in religious settings to ensure that a child or adolescent has oppor-

tunities to trust others, feel safe, experience adventure, feel valued, be heard and look forward to the future.[80]

7.5 *Meeting criteria of health and wholeness*

Because young people who have had difficult or distressing backgrounds require understanding and may be vulnerable, it is particularly important that the faith community of their own religious persuasion, or that which welcomes them, is so far as possible a main religious faith with a healthy local faith community.

Faith community health and wholeness requires the following factors:

1. A faith community should have a membership which, in general, is reasonably balanced in gender, age range, circumstances and social class, and is welcoming to those of racial difference and also to visitors. Whilst this may not always be evident because of the particular situation or location of a local faith community, the disposition of breadth, balance and warmth for all should exist. The ethos of the faith community should be marked by a high standard of pastoral care, and its life should include social activities. These factors correlate with human spirituality.

2. A faith community should have a sincerity and authenticity of worship – of a style which is reverent, natural and culturally appropriate. In addition, it should be of a tradition which is historic and wider than the local faith community alone, and which gives due accountability to the larger faith community of which it is a part. It should not be oppressively rigid so as to engender fear, nor narrowly exclusive so as to be condemnatory of non-members. A faith community should also have a form of ministry or leadership which has regard for the spiritual gifts of all the members, which encourages the participation of its members, and which celebrates supportively and appropriately major and minor rites of passage. These factors correlate with devotional spirituality.

3. A faith community should have concern for its collective engagement, and the engagement of its members, with everyday life and with the wider world. It should also have concern for positive personal relationships, for health, for happiness and mutuality in family life, for overcoming problems, for social

responsibility and for the concerns of those (especially the young) with special difficulties or needs. A faith community needs to act upon these concerns, within moderation, and to have a sense of hope and resolve for the future. These factors correlate with practical spirituality.

Where a child or young person has no expressed religious persuasion, a welcoming faith community should be scrupulous not to exert any pressure or expectation about membership, but to support the child or young person as much as possible and to extend to them unconditionally the hospitality of fellowship and worship as required.

It should be pointed out that small sects and cults may be attractive to vulnerable young people, and perhaps particularly to those leaving care, because they can offer an immediate and heightened sense of 'belonging'. However, the wisdom, pastoral experience, spiritual depth and tested traditions of the main world faiths – to one of which the child or young person may naturally belong by virtue of his or her religious identity – should be reinforced by all concerned as being of life-long value and of availability across the country and throughout the world.

Eileen Barker, in a book which is to be strongly recommended not only for its overview of new religious movements, but for her discussion of family and parental factors arising from these, states that there are no less than 600 new religious movements in Britain today.[81] It follows from this that for a young person to receive no help, guidance or assurance about his or her own religious identity could be to expose them to a market place of groups and movements for which they could not readily be prepared.

CONCLUSION

It has been demonstrated that the spirituality of a child or young person describes a healthy attitude towards and pattern of engagement with themselves and their family, with their God and their faith community, and with their day-to-day activities and involvement with others in the wider world.

Put more formally, the distinction has been made between human, devotional and practical spirituality. Human spirituality is related to every child's need for love, security, reflection, praise and responsibility. The natural and appropriate fulfilment of these needs should be recognised and protected by society and schools. Devotional spirituality builds directly upon human spirituality and is generally to be expressed in the culture and language of a particular religion. Faith communities have a duty to nurture this in all their members, and care professionals should support this. Practical spirituality combines both human and devotional spirituality and is expressed in our day-to-day living, giving shape and direction to our lives' goals and to our social concerns and duties.

The argument put forward in this book has been that for a human being, especially a child or young person, to have a full quality of life, spirituality in all its aspects must be nurtured and affirmed. For children or young people who have been marginalised or who have suffered deprivation in any way, the need for such nurture and affirmation in human spirituality is all the more pronounced.

The thoughtful parent, care professional or teacher must always consider the tripartite spiritual needs of the child and support or seek resources for supporting them. Young people who have had no experience of devotional spirituality may be at risk of being pressured to fill the vacuum with spurious substitutes.

A totally new approach towards spirituality is therefore urgently necessary, which starts with supporting a child's human spirituality, respecting and enabling his or her devotional spirituality, and encouraging and welcoming his or her practical spirituality – and which goes on to see the progressive, and cyclical, interconnection between these. Spiritual development is not a secondary or disposable part of personal development but the essence of it, and no part of it can be arbitrarily excluded without significant loss.

It is important to remember that children and young people, whatever their background and circumstances, face the full challenges of living in today's world. Taken to its ultimate, practical spirituality involves meeting the goals of life as described by Laurens van der Post.[82]

> We now are bound to decide for ourselves consciously what is good and what is bad: to make what is meaningful take precedence over what is meaningless. It is the sense of this power, this sense of responsibility that we share with our creator; this sense of belonging to the universe that we have lost and that we must rediscover and embrace in a lasting act of remembrance of our origin to set ourselves and our societies once more on course.

A holistic spirituality should enable us to look forward in hope.

APPENDIX 1

Chart showing spirituality as a tripartite and holistic concept (with aspects of interiority in italics)

---

1. **Human spirituality** – wholeness of emotional, cognitive and intuitive self

a Receiving love and affection

b Security

c New experiences: (i) external, e.g. play and exploration; (ii) *internal, opportunities for inner stillness, awe and wonder*

d Receiving praise and recognition

e Opportunities to participate and take responsibility

---

2. **Devotional spirituality** – formation of corporate and personal religious life

a Religious identity and warmth of membership

b Security of established creed and moral code

c Possibilities for growth and discovery (i) in worship and scriptural tradition; (ii) *in the formation of an inner devotional life*

d Support of pastoral encouragement and intercession

e Multiple opportunities for taking part and serving others

---

3. **Practical spirituality** – engagement in personal and public everyday living

a A capacity for friendship and humanity of interaction

b A capacity for coping constructively with difficulty and dissonance

c A capacity for both (i) endeavour and enquiry; (ii) *reverence and reflection*

d A capacity for confidence in being open to growth and self-development, and in promoting development of others

e A capacity for an appreciation of community, and for a sense of social responsibility

---

APPENDIX 2

(Some sections are incomplete.)

1. (1) When a court determines any question with respect to —
   (a) the upbringing of a child; or
   (b) the administration of a child's property or the application
       of any income arising from it,
       the child's welfare shall be the court's paramount
       consideration.

(2) In any proceedings in which any question with respect to the upbringing of a child arises, the court shall have regard to the general principle that any delay in determining the question is likely to prejudice the welfare of the child.

(3) In the circumstances mentioned in subsection (4), a court shall have regard in particular to —
   (a) the ascertainable wishes and feelings of the child concerned (considered in the light of his age and understanding);
   (b) his physical, emotional and educational needs;
   (c) the likely effect on him of any change in his circumstances;
   (d) his age, sex, background and any characteristics of his which the court considers relevant;
   (e) any harm which he has suffered or is at risk of suffering;
   (f) how capable each of his parents, and any other person in relation to whom the court considers the question to be relevant, is of meeting his needs;
   (g) the range of powers available to the court under this Act in the proceedings in question.

22. (4) Before making any decision with respect to a child whom they are looking after, or proposing to look after, a local authority shall, so far as is reasonably practicable, ascertain the wishes and feelings of —
   (a) the child;
   (b) his parents;
   (c) any person who is not a parent of his but who has parental

responsibility for him; and

(d) any other person whose wishes and feelings the authority consider to be relevant,

regarding the matter to be decided.

(5) In making any such decision a local authority shall give due consideration —

(a) having regard to his age and understanding, to such wishes and feelings of the child as they have been able to ascertain;

(b) to such wishes and feelings of any person mentioned in sub-section (4)(b) to (d) as they have been able to ascertain; and

(c) to the child's religious persuasion, racial origin and cultural and linguistic background.

24. — (1) Where a child is being looked after by a local authority, it shall be the duty of the authority to advise, assist and befriend him with a view to promoting his welfare when he ceases to be looked after by them.[83]

APPENDIX 3

A selected list of useful references to religious care in 'The Children Act 1989: Guidance and Regulations'

Volume 3: Family Placements

Section
2.5	for full consideration as part of welfare
2.21	identifying appropriate provision
2.49–42	religious background
2.51(e)	potential for consultation in planning
2.62	identified religious needs as a key element of placement plan
3.24	assessment of fostering enquirers
4.4–5	continuity in religious/church life
4.12	information to foster parents
7.10	independent visitor
8.11(viii)	consultation in reviews
8.20	on religious provision in review
9.46	volunteer adult befrienders
9.52,3	young person's self-esteem
9.55	finding and using community resources

Volume 4: Residential Care

Section
1.20	statement of values and ethos of a home
1.121–124	religious observance
1.129	catering arrangements
1.146	dress
1.153	implicit provision for religious items in records
2.5	welfare
2.21	identifying appropriate religious provision
2.40–42	considering religious background
2.51(e)	potential for consultation
2.56	assessment
2.62	identified religious needs as a key element of placement plan

2.81	implicitly includes religious certificates
3.11(viii)	potential for consultation in review
3.19	on religious provision in review
5.9	possible potential for complaint
6.15	independent visitor
6.18	independent visitor recruitment
7.18	preparation for leaving care (item 6)
7.46	religion of befriender
7.52	self-esteem
7.53	counselling and religious matching
7.55	finding and using community resources
8.47	secure accommodation and welfare
9.7	refuges and welfare
page 139	Statutory Instruments (1991) No. 1506, sections 11, 12 on religious observance, and food provided for children and cooking facilities

APPENDIX 4

Extracts from the Education Reform Act 1988

(Some sections are incomplete.)

Duties with respect to the curriculum.

1.— (1) It shall be the duty —

(a) of the Secretary of State as respects every maintained school;

(b) of every local education authority as respects every school maintained by them; and

(c) of every governing body or head teacher of a maintained school as respects that school;

to exercise their functions (including, in particular, the functions conferred on them by this Chapter with respect to religious education, religious worship and the National Curriculum) with a view to securing that the curriculum for the school satisfies the requirements of this section.

(2) The curriculum for a maintained school satisfies the requirements of this section if it is a balanced and broadly based curriculum which —

(a) promotes the spiritual, moral, cultural, mental and physical development of pupils at the school and of society; and

(b) prepares such pupils for the opportunities, responsibilities and experiences of adult life.

Religious education

Collective worship.

6.— (1) Subject to section 9 of this Act, all pupils in attendance at a maintained school shall on each school day take part in an act of collective worship.

(2) The arrangements for the collective worship in a school required by this section may, in respect of each school day, provide for a single act of worship for all pupils or for separate acts of worship for pupils in different age groups or in different school groups.

(3) The arrangements for the collective worship in a county or voluntary school required by this section shall be made —

(a) in the case of a county school, by the head

teacher after consultation with the governing body; and

(b) in case of a voluntary school, by the governing body after consultation with the head teacher.

Special provisions as to collective worship in county schools.

7.— (1) Subject to the following provisions of this section, in the case of a county school the collective worship required in the school by section 6 of this Act shall be wholly or mainly of a broadly Christian character.

(2) For the purposes of subsection (1) above, collective worship is of a broadly Christian character if it reflects the broad traditions of Christian belief without being distinctive of any particular Christian denomination.

(3) Every act of collective worship required by section 6 of this Act in the case of a county school need not comply with subsection (1) above provided that, taking any school term as a whole, most such acts which take place in the school do comply with that subsection.

(4) Subject to subsections (1) and (3) above —

(a) the extent to which (if at all) any acts of collective worship required by section 6 of this Act which do not comply with subsection (1) above take place in a county school;

(b) the extent to which any act of collective worship in a county school which complies with subsection (1) above reflects the broad traditions of Christian belief; and

(c) the ways in which those traditions are reflected in any such act of collective worship;

shall be such as may be appropriate having regard to any relevant considerations relating to the pupils concerned which fail to be taken into account in accordance with subsection (5) below.

(5) Those considerations are —

(a) any circumstances relating to the family backgrounds of the pupils concerned which are relevant for determining the character of the collective worship which is appropriate in their case; and

(b) their ages and aptitudes.

(6) Where under section 12 of this Act a standing advisory council on religious education determine that it is not appropriate for subsection (1) above to apply in the case of any county school,

or in the case of any class or description of pupils at such a school, then, so long as that determination has effect —

(a) that subsection shall not apply in relation to that school or (as the case may be) in relation to those pupils; and

(b) the collective worship required by section 6 of this Act in the case of that school or those pupils shall not be distinctive of any particular Christian or other religious denomination (but this shall not be taken as preventing that worship from being distinctive of any particular faith).

Religious education required in the basic curriculum: further provisions.

8.— (1) Section 2(1)(a) of this Act is subject to section 9 of this Act.

(2) The religious education for which provision is required by section 2(1)(a) to be included in the basic curriculum for any particular maintained school shall be religious education of the kind required by such of the provisions of sections 26 to 28 of the 1944 Act or sections 84 to 86 of this Act as apply in the case of that school.

(3) Any agreed syllabus which after this section comes into force is adopted or deemed to be adopted under Schedule 5 to that Act (which, as amended by this Act, provides for the preparation, adoption and reconsideration of an agreed syllabus of religious education) shall reflect the fact that the religious traditions in Great Britain are in the main Christian whilst taking account of the teaching and practices of the other principal religions represented in Great Britain.

Exceptions, special arrangements and supplementary and consequential provisions.

9.— (1) It shall not be required, as a condition of any pupil attending any maintained school, that he shall attend or abstain from attending any Sunday school or any place of religious worship.

(2) For the purposes of subsections (3) to (10) below "maintained school" does not include a maintained special school.

(3) If the parent of any pupil in attendance at any maintained school requests that he may be wholly or partly excused —

(a) from attendance at religious worship in the school;

(b) from receiving religious education given in the school in accordance with the school's basic curriculum; or

(c) both from such attendance and from receiving such education;

the pupil shall be so excused accordingly until the request is withdrawn.

(4) Where in accordance with subsection (3) above any pupil has been wholly or partly excused from attendance at religious worship or from receiving religious education in any school, and the responsible authority are satisfied —

(a) that the parent of the pupil desires him to receive religious education of a kind which is not provided in the school during the periods of time during which he is so excused;

(b) that the pupil cannot with reasonable convenience be sent to another maintained school where religious education of the kind desired by the parent is provided; and

(c) that arrangements have been made for him to receive religious education of that kind during school hours elsewhere;

the pupil may be withdrawn from the school during such periods of time as are reasonably necessary for the purpose of enabling him to receive religious education in accordance with the arrangements.

(5) In this section "the responsible authority" means —

(a) in relation to a county or voluntary school, the local education authority; and

(b) in relation to a grant-maintained school, the governing body.

(6) A pupil may not be withdrawn from school under subsection (4) above unless the responsible authority are satisfied that the arrangements there mentioned are such as will not interfere with the attendance of the pupil at school on any day except at the beginning or end of the school session or, if there is more than one, of any school session on that day.[84]

References

1. The human spirituality of the child

1. Pringle, M.K. (1980) *The Needs of Children*. Hutchinson, 2nd Edition, chapter 2.

2. National Council of Voluntary Child Care Organisations. (1994) *Statement of Values and Principles in Working with Children, Young People and Families.*

3. Barclay, P. (Chairman). (1982) *Social Workers, Their Role and Tasks.* Report of a Working Party set up in October 1980 at the request of the Secretary of State for Social Services. National Institute for Social Work, p. 64, section 4.40.

4. Ignatieff, M. (1990) *The Needs of Strangers.* The Hogarth Press, p. 28.

5. United Nations Department of Public Information, New York. (1991) Convention on the Rights of the Child.

6. Berger, P.L. (1971) *A Rumour of Angels: Modern Society and the Rediscovery of the Supernatural.* Pelican, p. 76 and chapter 3.

7. Sacks, J. (1995) *Faith in the Future.* Darton, Longman and Todd, pp. 22–23.

8. Kirkland, J. (1994) *Helping to Restore Spiritual Values in Abused Children: A Role for Pastoral Carers in Education.* Paper for the conference on 'Spirituality and the Whole Child.' Froebel Institute, July.

9. Phillips, M. (1995) 'Family Planning.' *The Observer* ©. *Search.* Joseph Rowntree Foundation, Issue 22, Spring.

10. Dominian, J. (1991) *Passionate and Compassionate Love: A Vision for Christian Marriage.* Darton, Longman and Todd, p. 230.

11. Bloom, Metropolitan, A. (1986) 'Respecting Others.' *Children Worldwide.* Geneva: International Catholic Child Bureau, vol. 13, no. 2–3.

2. The devotional spirituality of the child

12. Brabant, F. (1954) 'Worship in General.' W.K. Lowther Clarke (Ed). *Liturgy and Worship.* SPCK.

13. Shelly, J.A. et al. (1984) *Spiritual Needs of Children.* Scripture Union.

14. Neville, G.K., Westerhoff, J.H. III. (1978) *Learning Through Liturgy.* New York: Seabury Press, chapter 8.

15. National Society and Church House Publishing. (1991) *How Faith Grows: Faith Development and Christian Education*, p. 52.

16. Neville, G.K., Westerhoff, J.H. III. (1978) *Learning Through Liturgy.* New York: Seabury Press, p. 169.

17. Bryars, G., Wallis, T. (1993) 'Jesus' Blood Never Failed Me Yet'. Compact single. Point Music.

18. Bion, W.R. (1970) *Attention and Interpretation.* Tavistock.

19. Crompton, M. (1992) *Children and Counselling.* Edward Arnold, chapters 7–10.

3. The practical spirituality of the child

20. Anglican Diocese of Lichfield. (1992) *Children: The Churches Care.* Policy guidelines, November.

21. HRH The Prince of Wales. (1989) *A Vision of Britain: A Personal View of Architecture.* Doubleday, p. 149.

22. Vanier, J. (1985) *Man and Woman He Made Them.* Darton, Longman and Todd, chapter 5.

23. Sacks, J. (1991) *The Persistence of Faith: Religion, Morality and Society in a Secular Age.* The BBC Reith Lectures, 1990. Weidenfeld and Nicolson, p. 106.

24. Skynner, R., Cleese, J. (1993) *Life and How to Survive It.* London: Methuen, pp. 33–34.

25. The Tavistock Institute of Marital Studies. (1995) *Something to Celebrate: Valuing Families in Church and Society.* The report of a Working Party by the Board for Social Responsibility of the General Synod of the Church of England. Church House Publishing, p. 162.

26. Loesel, Dr F. (1994) 'Protective factors which can bolster resilience'. *ICCB News.* New York: International Catholic Child Bureau, no. 1, p. 2.

27. Vanistendael, S. (1995) *Growth in the Muddle of Life: Resilience – Building on People's Strengths.* Geneva: International Catholic Child Bureau.

28. Lamb, C. (1985) *Belief in a Mixed Society.* Lion Publishing plc, chapter 8.

29. Westerhoff, J.H. III. (1973) *Will Our Children Have Faith?* New York: Seabury Press, p. 89.

30. Jung, C.G. (1933) *Modern Man in Search of a Soul*. Kegan Paul, p. 264.

31. Bryant, C. (1983) *Jung and the Christian Way*. Darton, Longman and Todd, p. 107.

32. Inner Cities Religious Council, London. *ICRC Profile: What is the Inner Cities Council?*

33. Fung, R. © (1992) *The Isaiah Vision: An Ecumenical Strategy for Congregational Evangelism*. Geneva: World Council of Churches Publications, p. 2.

34. Clarke, P. (1988) 'Introduction to New Religious Movements.' S. Sutherland, P. Clarke (Eds). *The Study of Religion, Traditional and New Religion*. Routledge, p. 152.

4. The inter-relationship of the three spiritualities

35. Mellaby, A.R., Phelps, F.A., Chrichton, N.J., Tripp, J.H. (1995) 'School Sex Education: An Experimental Programme with Educational and Medical Benefit'. *British Medical Journal,* no. 7002, vol. 311, 12 August, p. 416.

36. British Council of Churches. (1981) *Understanding Christian Nurture,* section 142.

37. Davie, G. (1994) *Religion in Britain Since 1945: Believing Without Belonging*. Blackwell.

38. Hasler, J. (1995) 'Belonging and Becoming: The Child Growing Up in Community.' P. Henderson (Ed). *Children and Communities*. Pluto Press, p. 173.

5. Implications for social work

39. Department of Health. (1991) *The Children Act 1989: Guidance and Regulations: Volume 3, Family Placements* and *Volume 4, Residential Care*. HMSO.

40. Wyld, N. *Living Away From Home: Your Rights*. A guide for children and young people, the Children Act; CAG7. The Department of Health, p. 24.

41. Religious Resource and Education Centre. (1995). *Religions in the UK: A Multi-Faith Directory*. University of Derby and the Inter-Faith Network UK.

42. Chase, Revd R. (1995) 'A Child's Image of God: The Roots of Resilience'. *ICCB News*. International Catholic Child Bureau's North American Regional Office, Special Edition, pp. 10–11.

43. Portsmouth Diocesan Council for Social Responsibility. *Concise Guide to the Customs of Ethnic Minority Religions in Hampshire.*

44. Promoting Christian Child Care Alternatives. *Children Act 1989: Day Care of Children under 8 Years of Age.*

45. Biestek, F.P. (1961) *The Casework Relationship.* George Allen and Unwin, p. 116.

46. Special Religious Education Division, Archdiocese of Chicago. *SPRED.* Monthly newsletter.

47. Muller-Fahrenholz, G. (1979) *Partners in Life: The Handicapped and the Church.* World Council of Churches.

48. World Council of Churches Office of Family Education. (1981) *Report of Consultation on Humanity and Wholeness of Persons with Disabilities.* Sao Paulo, Brazil, November.

49. Working Group on the Religious Life of the Disabled Person, London. (1982) *Disabled People in the Church: Some Conclusions from the International Year for Disabled People.* International Year for Disabled People, UK.

50. Ahsan, M.M. (1992) Preface to T. Yawar, *Caring about Faith.* Leicester: The Islamic Foundation.

51. Paraiso, A., Mayled, J. (1987) *Soul Cakes and Shish Kebabs: A Multifaith Cookery Book.* Religious and Moral Education Press.

52. Neuberger, J. (1994) *Caring for Dying People of Different Faiths.* Meditec Booksellers.

53. Department of Health Dartington Social Research Unit. (1995) *Looking After Children: Assessment and Action Records* (Age Under One Year; Age One and Two Years; Age Three and Four Years; Age Five to Nine Years; Age Ten to Fourteen years; Age Fifteen Years and Over).

54. Ward, H. (Ed). (1995) *Looking After Children: Research into Practice.* The second report of the Department of Health on assessing outcomes in child care. HMSO, p. 170.

55. Colton, M., Drury, C., Williams, M. 'Policies on Ethnic, Linguistic and Religious Needs in Wales Under the Children Act 1989.' *Social Work and Social Sciences Review*, vol. 5(1), p. 61.

6. Implications for education

56. Dearing, R. (1994) *The National Curriculum and its Assessment.* School Curriculum and Assessment Authority, December, section 3.33.

57. National Curriculum Council. (1993) *Spiritual and Moral Development,* April.

58. Office for Standards in Education. (1994) *Spiritual, Moral, Social and Cultural Development.* Ofsted, p. 8, section 2.1.

59. The Islamic Academy, Cambridge. (1993) *Spiritual and Moral Development: A response to the NCC Discussion Paper,* pp. 6–7.

60. Department of Education. (1994) *Religious Education and Collective Worship.* Department of Education Circular 94/81, January.

61. Hull, J.M. (1975) *School Worship: An Obituary.* SCM Press, pp. 132–134.

62. Pyke, N. (1994) '"Worship" the Key to Assembly Problems.' *Times Educational Supplement,* 4 November.

63. Bradford, J. (1987) 'Worship Assembly in the Multi-Faith School: A Proposal for a New Approach.' *Discernment.* A Christian journal of inter-religious encounter. The Committee for Relations with People of Other Faiths, British Council of Churches, vol. 2, no. 2, p. 17.

64. Lindley, R. (1992) 'The common factor.' *Education,* 28 August.

65. Walker, M. (1986) 'Human and Spiritual Development.' A. Ecclestone, P. Sheldrake, M. Walker, G. Wakefield, *Spirituality and Human Wholeness.* British Council of Churches, p. 50.

66. Fowler, J.W. (1976) *Stages of Faith.* New York: Harper Row.

67. Wordsworth, W. (1939) 'Ode on the Intimations of Immortality from Recollections of Early Childhood.' Sir A. Quiller-Couch, *The Oxford Book of English Verse 1250–1918.* Oxford University Press, New Edition, p. 628.

68. Heller, D. (1986) *The Children's God.* University of Chicago Press, p. 151.

69. Sacks, J. (1991) *The Persistence of Faith: Religion, Morality and Society in a Secular Age.* The BBC Reith lectures, 1990. Weidenfeld and Nicolson, p. 93.

70. Prentice, E.A. (1995) 'Sudanese Christians Sold as Slaves.' *The Times,* 25 August.

71. Mitchell, P.J. (1994) 'Can Education Have a Religious Foundation Today?: A Christian View.' S.A. Ashraf, P.H. Hirst, *Religion and Education: Islamic and Christian Approaches.* Cambridge: The Islamic Academy, p. 27.

7. Implications for faith communities

72. The Committee for Relations with People of Other Faiths. (1991) *In Good Faith: The Four Principles of Interfaith Dialogue.* A brief guide

for the Churches. Council of Churches for Britain and Ireland, section 7.

73. The InterFaith Network for the United Kingdom. *Building Good Relations with People of Different Faiths.*

74. Gagnon, Cardinal E. (1994) 'The Child is Also the Future of the Church'. *The Child is the Future of Society: Proceedings of the Eighth International Conference Organised by the Pontifical Council for Pastoral Assistance to Health Care Workers.* Dolentium Hominum, Vatican City, p. 140.

75. de Giorgi, S. 'The Child in Christian Culture', Toaff, E. 'Jewish Culture', Tantamy, M.S. 'The Protection of Children and Islamic Law', Nu Cha Duc, T. 'Buddhist Culture', Sahdev, K. 'The Child in Indian Culture'. *The Child is the Future of Society.* Dolentium Hominum, Vatican City.

76. The Consultative Group on Ministry among Children. (1995) *Unfinished Business: Children and the Churches.* Council for Churches in Britain and Ireland, section 1.1 ff.

77. Catholic Institute for International Relations (1980) *Puebla: Evangelisation at Present and in the Future of Latin America – Conclusions.* General Conference of Latin American Bishops, 1979. Slough: St Paul Publications, and London: CIIR.

78. Ward, H. (Ed). (1995) *Looking after Children: Research into Practice.* The second report of the Department of Health on assessing outcomes in child care. HMSO, p. 56.

79. Exeter Diocese Children and Young People's Commitee. (1995) *Links,* Summer, p. 2.

80. Bradford, J. (1994) 'Spiritual and Religious Rights of Children.' *Children Worldwide.* Geneva: International Catholic Child Bureau, vol. 21, no. 1, p. 20.

81. Barker, E. (1989) *New Religious Movements: A Practical Introduction.* HMSO, Fourth Impression with amendments, 1995, p. 165.

Conclusion

82. Van der Post, L. (1988) *A Walk with a White Bushman.* Penguin, p. 83.

Appendices

83. Crown copyright. Children Act 1989.

84. Crown copyright. Education Reform Act 1988.